SAGE was founded in 1965 by Sara Miller McCune to support the dissemination of usable knowledge by publishing innovative and high-quality research and teaching content. Today, we publish over 900 journals, including those of more than 400 learned societies, more than 800 new books per year, and a growing range of library products including archives, data, case studies, reports, and video. SAGE remains majority-owned by our founder, and after Sara's lifetime will become owned by a charitable trust that secures our continued independence.

Los Angeles | London | New Delhi | Singapore | Washington DC | Melbourne

ADVANCE PRAISE

Sujit is amongst a rare breed of analytical writers with an unparalleled command of three critical components—the food chain, agricultural technology and economics. The book is an easy-to-read narrative with anecdotes and international best practices combined with a deep dive into the psyche of rural India and a farm-to-fork agritech strategy. Undisputedly, India is on the cusp of an agricultural revolution, so this is a compelling read for anyone interested in the future of India.

Deepak Parekh, *Chairman,*
Housing Development Finance Corporation, India

A Wall Street View of Rural India established Sujit Sahgal as a researcher with his eye on the hoi polloi. The two newbies of 21st century agriculture—youth and agritech, introduced in this book's last section—find robust wings in the author's succeeding book, *Agribusiness and Technology.*

The role of these two actors in reshaping agriculture as an agribusiness is well substantiated. The well-tested 'Sahgal methodology' of integrating secondary with primary data helps in generating a froth of ground-truth insights.

A must-read for all those aspiring to understand new India's future of farming, assuring you that you will love to read it for its ease and lucidity.

Dr Ashok Dalwai,
CEO, National Rainfed Area Authority,
and Chairman, Empowered Body,
Doubling Farmers' Income, Ministry of Agriculture and
Farmers' Welfare, Government of India

While the problems facing Indian agriculture are well documented and understood, Sujit Sahgal brings a refreshing 'on-the-ground and on-the-farm' perspective to them by going to the grassroots and taking inputs from farmers across the country to understand what will work for them and what will not. This approach makes this book differentiated as it touches upon a very large number of issues, from global experiences to the local landscape, and brings out new and actionable ideas on the use of agritech and best practices for farmers. Its story-like approach also ensures that it will find resonance with stakeholders, including farmers, agribusinesses, academia and policymakers. It is indeed good to see non-agricultural professionals taking a keen interest in this subject.

Suresh Narayanan,
Chairman and Managing Director,
Nestle India

Technology is now all pervasive, and it is only a matter of time before it becomes an integral part of India's farming, even in those areas of agriculture in which there is not enough use of technology at present. Mr Sujit Sahgal's book is relevant to the future of Indian agriculture as it examines the pathways to the options available to make it viable for small farmers also. Anyone interested in the future of Indian agriculture will find this book interesting and relevant.

Siraj Hussain, *Visiting Senior Fellow, Indian Council for Research on International Economic Relations; Former Chairman of Food Corporation of India; Former Chief Secretary, Ministry of Agriculture, Government of India*

The issue of small farmers' livelihoods in India is challenging both in policy and practice. This concise and empirical book examines the appropriate role of technology in enabling

India's small farmers to earn a decent livelihood. Sujit is convincing in his argument that farm size is not an issue in the viability of farming. The book dwells on major issues ranging from land leasing to extension, sustainability, producer organization and inclusion. Sujit's style of weaving concepts and frameworks with short and relevant field-based stories makes the book very engaging for anyone keen on gaining a grounded understanding of globalized Indian agriculture.

Sukhpal Singh, *Professor and Chairperson,*
Centre for Management in Agriculture,
Indian Institute of Management, Ahmedabad

Sujit Sahgal's new book is a wonderful overview of the challenges facing farmers in India and how technology adoption can help transform Indian agriculture and food systems. Omnivore helped pioneer agritech investing in India over the past decade, and we are thrilled to see Sujit's insights regarding the potential of this sector. If you care about India's 13 crore farmers, read this book!

Mark Kahn, *Managing Partner, Omnivore*

It's rare to find an investment banker possessing a granular understanding of agriculture and also a passion for the sector. Sujit Sahgal has both. *Agribusiness and Technology* offers a grounded view of the challenges facing Indian agriculture—how to produce more with less input as well as environmental costs amid rising weather uncertainty. It also shows how new digital agriculture technologies can provide solutions by reducing drudgery and attracting our rural youth to stay back and scale up their family farm businesses.

Harish Damodaran, *National Rural Affairs and*
Agriculture Editor, The Indian Express;
Senior Fellow, Centre for Policy Research

AGRIBUSINESS AND TECHNOLOGY

SAGE Response, our business books imprint, celebrates its silver jubilee this year. As we reflect on this transformational journey that began with a single title, we thank everyone who has helped us to produce content that is topical and relevant across a varied audience of aspiring managers, working professionals, practitioners and students. We feel privileged that eminent management and leadership experts, professionals and stalwarts from academia supported and trusted us with their work. Over the years, SAGE Response has built an enviable list of practice-based, reader-friendly books that provide creative strategies to keep pace with the rapidly changing global scenario. As we grow and evolve with the times, it is our endeavour to continue to publish books that offer innovative solutions, approaches and perspectives to the disciplines that we serve.

AGRIBUSINESS AND TECHNOLOGY

Revolutionizing the Future of Farming

SUJIT SAHGAL

Los Angeles | London | New Delhi
Singapore | Washington DC | Melbourne

Copyright © Sujit Sahgal, 2022

All rights reserved. No part of this book may be reproduced or utilized in any form or by any means, electronic or mechanical, including photocopying, recording or by any information storage or retrieval system, without permission in writing from the publisher.

Disclaimer: The opinions and views expressed in this book are author's own and not of his employer.

First published in 2022 by

SAGE Publications India Pvt Ltd
B1/I-1 Mohan Cooperative Industrial Area
Mathura Road, New Delhi 110 044, India
www.sagepub.in

SAGE Publications Inc
2455 Teller Road
Thousand Oaks, California 91320, USA

SAGE Publications Ltd
1 Oliver's Yard, 55 City Road
London EC1Y 1SP, United Kingdom

SAGE Publications Asia-Pacific Pte Ltd
18 Cross Street #10-10/11/12
China Square Central
Singapore 048423

Published by Vivek Mehra for SAGE Publications India Pvt Ltd. Typeset in 11/14pt Sabon by Fidus Design Pvt Ltd, Chandigarh.

Library of Congress Cataloging-in-Publication Data
Name: Sahgal, Sujit, author.
Title: Agribusiness and technology: revolutionizing the future of farming / Sujit Sahgal.
Description: Thousand Oaks: SAGE Publishing, 2021.
Identifiers: LCCN 2021043960 | ISBN 9789354791901 (paperback) | ISBN 9789354791987 (epub) | ISBN 9789354792038 (ebook)
Subjects: LCSH: Agricultural industries—India. | Agriculture—Economic aspects—India. | Agriculture—India. | Alternative agriculture—India.
Classification: LCC HD9016.I42 S24 2021 | DDC 338.10954—dc23
LC record available at https://lccn.loc.gov/2021043960

ISBN: 978-93-5479-190-1 (PB)

SAGE Team: Namarita Kathait, Shruti Gupta and Anupama Krishnan

Dedicated to the loving memory of my father, the late Dhanraj Pershad Sahgal, who was always as curious as a teenager and never stopped learning. He instilled this hunger for knowledge in all of us.

To my mother, Shanta Sahgal, who being an educationist has taken so much interest in all my projects and shared my excitement.

To Veena, my dear wife, for her supreme confidence in me and willingness to hit the road and roll up her sleeves for meeting farmers with me whenever I had to.

And to Saaz and Swar, my darling sons, who motivate me to keep exploring new paths and breaking new boundaries.

Thank you for choosing a SAGE product!
If you have any comment, observation or feedback,
I would like to personally hear from you.

Please write to me at **contactceo@sagepub.in**

Vivek Mehra, Managing Director and CEO, SAGE India.

Bulk Sales

SAGE India offers special discounts
for purchase of books in bulk.
We also make available special imprints
and excerpts from our books on demand.

For orders and enquiries, write to us at

Marketing Department
SAGE Publications India Pvt Ltd
B1/I-1, Mohan Cooperative Industrial Area
Mathura Road, Post Bag 7
New Delhi 110044, India

E-mail us at **marketing@sagepub.in**

Subscribe to our mailing list

Write to marketing@sagepub.in

This book is also available as an e-book.

CONTENTS

Foreword by Dinesh Kumar Khara ix
Preface xiii
Acknowledgements xvii

Part I: Framing the Problem and the Solution 1
    Chapter 1: In Search of a SOLID
                   Farming Model 3
    Chapter 2: Beating the Size Problem 19

Part II: The Who and How of Farming 37
    Chapter 3: Who Will Run the Farms? 39
    Chapter 4: How Will They Run It? 53

Part III: Understanding Agritech: The Old and
          the New 63
    Chapter 5: Towards a Broad Definition
                   of Technology in Agriculture 65
    Chapter 6: Slicing and Dicing Technology 83

Part IV: Lay of the Land: A Global and Indian
          Perspective 95
    Chapter 7: Mapping the Global
                   Agritech Landscape 97
    Chapter 8: The Indian Agritech Landscape 119
    Chapter 9: What the Government Is Doing
                   and Where It Should Focus 139

Part V: Ground Stories and Farmer Inputs 159
    Chapter 10: What the Farmer Knows
                    and Thinks 161
    Chapter 11: Understanding the Farmer's
                    Pain Points and Looking
                    for the Sweet Spot 173

Part VI:	Closing the Loop with All Stakeholders Together	183
	Chapter 12: Bridging the Gaps and Providing a Pathway	185
	Chapter 13: A Marriage Made on Earth	199
	Chapter 14: How Modern Methods Can Change Agriculture Forever	207

Appendix: More Ground Stories — 219
About the Author — 235

FOREWORD

It has been my pleasure to know Sujit Sahgal as a friend and fellow banker. His banking career of over 25 years in the financial markets is primarily in macro strategy, sector and company research and global investments. I am happy that his flair for research in banking has led him to author this book as a follow-on to *A Wall Street View of Rural India*, published last year.

The book's theme is a specialized one within agriculture, but Sujit's attempt is unpretentious and very realistic. He has attempted to analyse the problem, delineate the solutions and present the view not from the armchair but from the ground, from the fields of India—Kashmir to Kerala, Gandhidham to the Dibang Valley. The stories that he weaves are what make this book relevant and different. Rich as it is with data and facts, the pages come alive because they speak directly from the village of Theog in Himachal, 'on a chilly December afternoon', or from Dehradun, highlighting the menace of monkeys wreaking havoc on the crop of lemons, rice and pulses.

We have witnessed tremendous strides made by the Indian agriculture sector, thanks to the assiduous work of our farmers and the brilliant research contributions of our farm scientists. We now live in an era of plenty. India is an exporter of rice and wheat and the largest producer of cotton and milk in the world, to mention just a few of our achievements. More recently, we have seen how our agriculture sector has recorded positive output growth even during 2020–2021, when all other sectors recorded negative growth and our economy, in effect, shrank along global trendlines. The farming community across our country once again demonstrated their resilience, ability to cope with challenging externalities and come up with positive outcomes, against all odds.

In agriculture, national discourse has focused on improving farmers' livelihoods. As early as in February 2016, the government articulated the target of 'doubling farmers' incomes' by 2022. This aspiration has caught the nation's imagination and led to a series of efforts by all the stakeholders—policymakers, farm scientists, financial intermediaries, regulators and the farming community itself.

Much ground has been covered in this journey and one very tangible, constructive move which comes to mind is the continuous increase in the minimum support prices (MSP) of agricultural commodities. The most popular agricultural produce, rice and wheat, have seen MSP increases of close to 40 per cent since 2015, while soyabean and cotton have recorded a rise of 50 per cent. This has been accompanied by higher procurement activities, and the farmers, on the whole, have benefited.

There are questions which occupy the minds of policymakers about taking agriculture and allied activities to the next level. How do we ensure that the small and marginal farmers, who constitute about 90 per cent of our farmer community, continue to remain engaged in agriculture and reach levels of development and standards of living comparable to those of people in other professions? How do we also improve the lives of millions of others who are also dependent on agriculture, like farm labourers? How can we utilize technology, both traditional and digital, to aid and guide the forward push for growth with greater equity in agriculture?

To my mind, technology is probably the only viable answer to pushing the frontiers of agriculture further.

No technical solution would mean anything to the farmer on the field unless it touches their lives in a meaningful and positive way. A fancy 'app' developed in the best 'garages' of the techie world may sometimes not make a whiff of a difference to the small farmer.

The test and touchstone of the utility of technology will have to be the fields of India. The centre of agritech, therefore, must be the small farmer, its radius and circumference their small strip of a field and the benefit, to be measured in terms of increases, at least incremental to the farmer's income.

Sujit attempts precisely this in his second offering. Framing issues related to agribusiness and technology, Sujit tries to explore attempts at providing technological solutions to the day-to-day problems and issues of farmers. This book is an interesting and refreshing read and could be of immense use to all stakeholders. Farmers, policymakers, scientists and techies can take cues from the book and contribute in their own way to resolution of the existing issues and achieve the coveted milestone of 'doubling farmers' income' by 2022.

Dinesh Kumar Khara,
Chairman, State Bank of India

PREFACE

It was the summer of 2020 when my first book *A Wall Street View of Rural India* had released amid the pandemic. Given the topic, there was a lot of interest in the agriculture circles in India, and I was getting several invitations to speak at forums and colleges. The last section of my book was devoted to the 'Future of Farming', and it focused on demographic changes and use of technology in farming and how that could be a very elegant, low-cost and sustainable solution to improve the farmers' income. One of the agriculture experts, who was reviewing my book at that time, mentioned to me that he really liked reading that section and found it very interesting and something which was not dealt in a lot of detail in Indian media. In many ways he sowed the seed in my mind of doing more work on that subject. Coincidentally, during the following months, there was a burst of media coverage on new agritech start-ups, and I also started commenting on the goings-on on my social media handles. As my fellow authors will agree, writing a book is addictive. You cannot stop at one! Hence, by the fall of 2020, I had started to seriously think about what I was going to write on next. And one chilly night in November, voila! I realized that the answer was right in front of me! In the morning, I woke up and told my wife that I had not only found the topic of my next book but also its title!—how agribusiness and technology can revolutionize the future of farming in India. And the book was born.

I started thinking through as to what I wanted the key message to be in the book. I realized that the topic was a specialized one within agriculture, and hence one will have to dive deep into the topic. But at the same time, I was clear that it had to appeal to the wider public in urban and rural India. The message had to spread wider. The other thing I was clear about was that it must be mainly primary research-driven, which was also the hallmark of my first book. It had to be a from-the-ground-up view coming from the farmers themselves.

There was so much information about agritech companies worldwide launching exotic products and services in the USA, Europe, Israel, Africa, India and China. I worried that so much information will overwhelm the farmers. Hence, the idea was to visit farmers—as many as I could, given the pandemic—and lay down the landscape in front of them in a simple language and highlight the most relevant pieces, but more importantly to understand their views and thoughts about agritech, gauge how much they already know, how curious they are to learn, and how able and willing they are to adopt these new methods and technologies. What do they need? Which part of the problem do they want to solve first? How does it have to be delivered to them? At what price point? and so on. One could then map the 'supply' of solutions (by the government and agribusinesses) with the 'demand' and look at the gaps, understand the low-hanging fruit and suggest a path to achieve rapid adoption of early and high-impact benefits—the only way to create the precious word of mouth. This really excited me. And I wanted to make sure that these conversations are shared with the readers as well. Hence, I decided to use the diary format, where every chapter started with a real-life story of a farmer or related person I met. This I believe will bring to life the points I want to make and take the reader on a virtual tour with me across the heartlands and farmlands of India.

I hope you will immerse yourself in this pan-India walk I take you through, from Kashmir to Kerala and Bihar to Gujarat, meeting the smallest farmer owning less than an acre to farmers owning hundreds of acres and others operating farms of thousands of acres, sharing with them what I knew, listening to their feedback and views, and gauging their curiosity, ability and willingness to change. This book is the story emerging from all these interactions. But this is equally a story of the immense and multipronged effort the governments, past and present, have put into this as well as the story of the mature and the start-up agri or agritech business. I have carefully curated their views as well. Because it is indeed true that a lasting solution will only emerge if all these three stakeholders work together. Agritech, I believe, is not only for the farmer to use or the agritech company to supply, or even just for the government to facilitate (which it is doing) but also for the government to use itself in policy design, implementation and monitoring and measuring of outcomes and compliance.

The book is divided into six parts with two–three chapters in each part. The first part deals with framing the problem and the solution framework. After which I dwell on the who and how of farming before moving into the third part, which is a very deep dive into what the various definitions of agritech are and the entire scope of technology, modern methods and best practices being followed. The fourth part then explains the global and local landscape in terms of what kind of companies are addressing which spaces within the value chain, what governments are doing globally and a chapter dedicated to what have been the policy, reform and focus of the Indian government as well. The fifth part is all about the farmer insights, and the sixth part ends with the mapping of the gaps, suggesting a pathway to achieve early, high-impact adoption and spreading the word.

It has been a truly enlightening and enriching journey that I am glad I took up. I am personally very optimistic and enthused about the future of Indian farming and improving economics of the farmers. I hope some of that I can rub off on my readers too!

ACKNOWLEDGEMENTS

First and foremost, I am grateful to Dr Siraj Hussain, the former secretary of Agriculture and Farmers' Welfare (GoI) and currently visiting senior fellow at Indian Council for Research on International Economic Relations (ICRIER). It was his feedback that set me on the path to explore this topic in more details.

I would like to thank Ritambhara Singh, associate professor at Dr Rajendra Prasad Central Agricultural University. She has been a constant help to me in locating the right sources of information and experts to talk to as well as sharing contacts of a lot of NGOs, farmer producer organizations (FPOs) and farmers. She never hesitated in helping me and encouraged me throughout this project.

I must mention Mr G. Chandrashekhar—an economist, senior journalist, agri-commodity expert and commentator—who has been a well-wisher, and his words of encouragement and belief in me have helped tremendously in giving me the confidence to take up this project.

I would also like to thank Benjamin Mathew and Dr Vinita Chaturvedi of MART, Pradeep Lokhande of Rural Relations, Nikhil Sharma of ITC e-Choupal and my childhood friend Umesh Nair, who were all kind enough to help me connect with people on the ground all over the country.

Finally, but most importantly, a big thanks to all those farmers, block development officers (BDOs), extension officers, FPOs, NGOs, KVK staff as well as agritech and agribusiness companies, that have taken out time to speak to me to share their invaluable insights and views. The rich mix of learning would not have been possible without that.

PART I

FRAMING THE PROBLEM AND THE SOLUTION

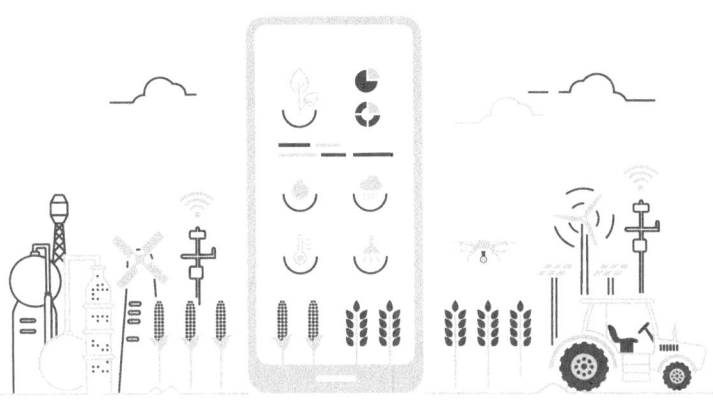

CHAPTER 1

IN SEARCH OF A SOLID FARMING MODEL

Ground-up Story: From Corn to Solar—So Different, Yet So Similar

While we were driving from New York to Chicago in the spring of 2021, we drove through the farm country of Pennsylvania. As planned, we stopped on the way and went in to meet one of the farmers. Mark was a jovial guy and did not mind us stopping by unannounced and asking him inquisitive questions. He had about 110 acres of farmland on which, primarily, corn and soybean were grown along with some vegetables. He told me that he did not operate the farm himself and had leased it out to his neighbours—the Johnsons—who did the cultivation on a combined piece of about 200 acres. Mark got a fixed fee without any variable component. He said that he had no family members who were interested in running it or had all grown old; hence, he leased it out. He told us that farming was quite profitable in his region, as water was plenty, power supply was cheap and consistent, and the soil was fertile. He also highlighted when I asked him about one *big* change he had seen in the recent past, and he said, 'no till farming', which helped them protect soil texture and fertility and prevented high amounts of erosion. I was very pleased to hear this, as I did not expect the very first farmer I met in the USA to bring up no-till, as it is one of the important things I will discuss in my book later.

While we thanked him and pulled away from the farm to continue our 15-hour drive to Chicago, Mark came up to me and said that he had just the previous day entered a new lease and that there would no longer be any farming on his land. He had leased his land to a solar farm operator who would generate solar power from panels. He almost sounded apologetic but said that it paid him much more than to lease it to his farmer neighbour!

I was very taken aback and a little sad too. Will countryside drives not be the same anymore? No more swaying corn ears! It also struck me, however, that despite such big differences between India and the USA (2-acre farms vs 200-acre farms), there were these similarities—no manpower to run the farm, so renting it out and leaving farming altogether in pursuit of more profitable avenues.

TRADITIONAL FARMING ON ITS LAST LEG

At the heart of agribusiness and technology is the focus on how these can revolutionize the future of farming. And there are many critical reasons why it needs to happen right now.

Taking a multi-decade view from now to 2050, the activity of farming is going to face several changes and challenges.

First, of the 7.8 billion people in the world, about 1 billion are already undernourished. Moreover, the world population is projected to increase by another 2 billion people by 2050 (to 9.9 billion),[1] which means materially more people to feed.

Second, income levels of people are going to increase along with GDP growth, which will in turn lead to higher purchasing power and higher consumption of food per capita but also a

[1] https://interactives.prb.org/2020-wpds/

disproportionate increase in certain kinds of food (protein-rich dairy, meats, etc.).

Third, accelerating climate change is causing more erratic weather and rains. With warmer weather and more droughts, yields are likely to be under pressure. Since 1990, in fact, yield improvements in the developed world have stalled primarily due to climate change, which offset other positive changes which took place.

Fourth, to add to this challenge, key agricultural resources—land and water—are both getting scarcer. There has only been an 8 per cent increase in arable land globally in the last 40 years,[2] while production has doubled. In fact, there has been no increase in arable land since 1990. Land acquisition by industries and trade zones is reducing arable land at an alarming pace in the developed world, and it will continue to do so also because the farmer is a willing seller as he grows older and the income from farming continues to be under pressure.

Fifth, as higher farming activity also leads to pollution (water, air and soil damage), the farmer is now being called upon to be environmentally efficient too, which is also adding to his cost. Seventy per cent of global water sources are used by agriculture, and twenty-four per cent of all greenhouse gases also come from agriculture.[3] While this is the global picture, the trends in India are not very different[4] with respect to population growth, arable land[5] and the degree of erratic climate. Figures 1.1 and 1.2 sum this up well.

---

[2] Course on 'Agriculture, Economics and Nature' by the University of Western Australia, offered on Coursera.
[3] https://openknowledge.worldbank.org/handle/10986/35216
[4] https://www.macrotrends.net/countries/IND/india/population
[5] https://data.worldbank.org/indicator/AG.LND.ARBL.HA?locations=IN

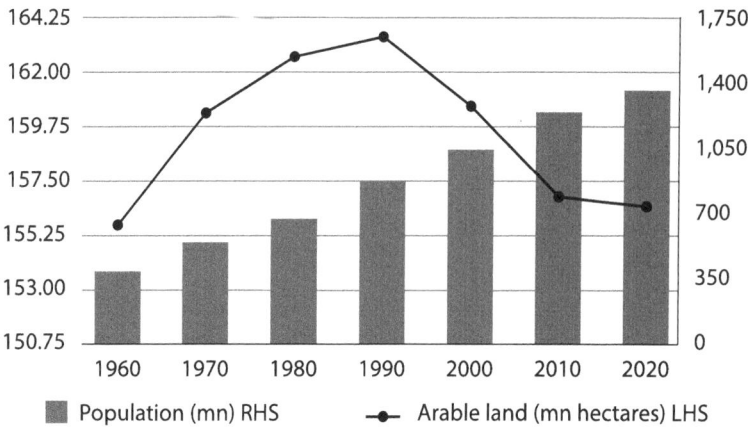

Figure 1.1. Rising Population and Dropping Arable Land in India

Source: Macrotrends.net; World Bank database.

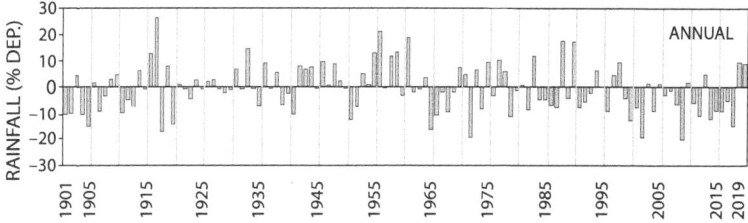

Figure 1.2. Time Series of All-India Annual Rainfall Percentage Departure (1901–2020)

Source: Indian Meteorological Department, 'Statement on Climate of India', 4 January 2021, https://www.imdpune.gov.in/Statement%20of%20Climate%20of%20India-2020.pdf

With all this, to increase agricultural output is a huge challenge for the farmers. They must produce more with less resources in more volatile weather and in an environment-friendly way. And, given the low income of the farmers, they have been exiting farming activity gradually, and hence this is a tall order for them to face. I think that it is clear therefore that the core farming activity needs to be very lucrative for the farmers to stick to farming, take up all these challenges and deliver the goods. This requires a meaningful increase in productivity and efficiency on the farm. While this continues to be done, partly, using better inputs (seeds, fertilizers and pesticides) and more mechanization, the use of technology has to play a much bigger role, especially in developed markets, where traditional methods have already been used a fair bit. In fact, as the farmers move against these various headwinds, it is clear that any big change in yields and productivity will now only come from the adoption of path-breaking technology. While the lower-middle income countries have more room to benefit from mechanization, traditional efficiency drivers and best practices, a deep adoption of technology is equally important. Just increasing fertilizer or pesticide usage is not the easy solution anymore, given the environment cost.

It is therefore not a surprise that governments world over (from China to the European Union, to the USA to India) are realizing the seriousness and urgency of reforming agriculture and learning that technology is not just a glamourous-sounding nice-to-have word which is floating around in venture capital (VC) circles but a necessity and the only way out to achieve *higher food production* in an *environmentally safe* way and keep the activity *profitable for the farmer*. Indeed, all agritech being used globally can be mapped as just solutions for these three problems. It is this important aspect of the need for farming to be profitable in a sustainable way for the farmer that I have picked up as my main approach and built the focus of this book around what I have called a *SOLID* farming model, which mainly focuses on a meaningful increase in the farmers' income on a sustainable basis.

INTRODUCTION TO 'SOLID'

It is always better to simplify complex concepts by putting acronyms around them. And it is even more pertinent with the complex topic we are dealing with. I strongly believe that, on the one hand, to address the above-mentioned food security and environment issues, farming activity must become inherently more profitable *but,* on the other hand, the evolution, availability and adoption of technology and modern methods in agriculture will also automatically enhance the farmers' profitability. Hence, technology is an elegant solution to meet the two important goals. Adoption of technology will lead to more profitable farming and that will then be the solution to the food security challenge because the well-earning farmer will be able to expand his production and bear the additional cost of adopting environment-friendly ways. This might be the only way, in fact. The fact is that even today, globally and in India, most of the farms are family-owned. Hence, if any of the above must be achieved, we need to keep the farmers and their future generations on the farm. A lasting way to achieve this is by making the core agricultural activity sustainably profitable on its own, that is, without needing constant help from the government (which cannot be everlasting from a fiscal perspective for any country) or from the weather (which is anyway getting more volatile globally). This is what I call the SOLID farming model or framework.

SOLID stands for Sustainable SOlutions for a Lucrative and Independent farming model, which helps to Double the farmers' income. I briefly expand on each of these below.

- **Sustainable solutions:** Here, I mean sustainable in two ways. One is from the environment perspective. Only if the activity is environmentally sustainable can it be carried out for the long run. Otherwise, eventually costs will get prohibitively high (soil erosion and water levels) or yields will start dropping (soil fertility). And the other is from a farmer's perspective. The solution has to be sustainable and long-lasting, not something tactical, which will work in a particular year or for certain given circumstances and not for others. The solution must make sense and come through in the long run and give consistently better returns. Only then will farmers embrace the changes needed. Sustainability is also important because many solutions for income enhancement usually tend to be ad hoc patchwork done by governments during times of need: higher-input subsidies, higher-procurement prices, bans on imports or exports, and the list goes on. A permanent long-term solution has to be found, and that is what the SOLID framework addresses.

- **Lucrative:** The agricultural activity has depended on so many variables such as weather and government policy and, even with basic mechanization, has remained hard physical work. Despite this, its rewards have been modest, not only in India but all over the world. Returns on effort may wary from country to country but are not the most attractive when compared to other opportunities that a farmer may have. Farmland owners even in the USA are leasing out their land to solar farms rather than to corn or bean farmers! Hence, making farming much more profitable is at the core of any solution. We must also understand the profitability of cultivation activity from a broader perspective, as this refers to the income of the farmers, not just the price of the crop they sell, but what they really earn from it after their costs. Again, it is not only the price of their crop but how many crops they are growing in a year (multicropping), the crops they are growing (crop selection), the yield, the costs, the loss and wastage, which all then add up to their income. It is important to appreciate all the aspects and define income in the broadest possible way. That will help us find more sustainable and easier-to-adopt solutions than if we focus on just one aspect of their income, which is the price, for example.

- **Independent:** By independent, I again mean two things: without dependence on the government or the weather. Both are easily said than done, but again very crucial and something which must be focused on.

The first one is the dependence on the government. Everywhere in the world, governments have stepped in to ensure minimum income levels to farmers by drawing a line in the sand. This is because food is an essential commodity. Farming has not been very lucrative on a consistent basis and is a highly fragmented activity, giving the farmer very low bargaining power.

The USA did it in the 1970s; Europe continues to do so; and India is no different in terms of providing support to its farmers. Whether it is price support or input help or protected market access or grants and subsidies or cheap loans, it comes in various shapes and sizes but amounts to the same thing—dependence on the government's fiscal capabilities. No government can have unlimited financial resources at its disposal, leave alone lower-middle income countries like India—even if there may be a lot of political will to do it. The other problem about government support is that the farmers get used to it. This is visible so often in my meetings with farmers—how much this dependence affects their critical decisions, what they grow and how they grow it being the most important casualty of extreme dependence. How they spend is another. If governments are going to consistently waive loans every few years, the incentive for farmers to build a sustainable, profitable business or even to put in more effort is low. Lastly, price guarantee schemes not only skew crop choice but also make the farmer far more risk averse and sometimes even lazy, not exploring crops and models which can help him to boost his income. So, in my opinion, it is critical to break this chain and demonstrate to the farmers that farming can be consistently and sustainably profitable without intermittent help from the government. In fact, there are several anecdotes which show that farmers who have shunned many government support schemes have actually done much better for themselves than those who have not because once government support gets pulled (which it inevitably will), the dependent farmers' business model will collapse. Most horticulture farmers are a classic case in point; with much lower support to that category by the government, they have built what they have, on their own, and hence it has been more sustainable. Similarly, younger farmers I have spoken to understand this and are shunning subsidies. Several grassroots workers I spoke to also had similar stories to share. I have shared more anecdotes throughout the book, which will highlight this point further.

The second is dependence on the weather. Only half of Indian arable land has irrigation coverage, which means that most farms are totally dependent on the rain, not just its quantity but also timing (early monsoons or unseasonal rains are as bad as late monsoons) and spatial distribution. Hence, even if India has experienced an above-normal monsoon in a year (defined as +/– 2% of the last 50-year average), it could still mean a very bad year for many farmers. Moreover, as we noted above, weather patterns are also shifting visibly, causing more erratic rain (more floods and droughts or even few days of torrential rain, coupled with large gaps of no rain), which is equally harmful. The point is that this weather uncertainty is here to stay, and it is going to get worse. So the farmers will have to have and adopt solutions and practices which reduce their dependence on rainfall. It is maybe impossible to delink completely, but they can reduce dependence materially, either by choosing crops which are hardy and need less water or by conserving water via harvesting or drip irrigation or precision techniques. Having the wrong kind of clusters for crops is a clear way of worsening the situation. Scientifically choosing the right crop for a particular region may be very difficult to orchestrate but can be a very powerful solution. Mulching, hydroponics, vertical farming and greenhouse farming are few more ways of partially or totally reducing dependence to the rains. They will be discussed and elaborated later on in the book.

- **Double their income:** All this must lead to material improvement in their income. I use the term 'double' here not to precisely fix a number but to express that directionally a *major* improvement can be achieved. I also do not fix a timeline (not the rolling target of five years governments often talk about in their manifestos) because the solutions that I talk about are not linear but step function changes which can be brought about immediately if the farmers can adopt disruptive changes to their practices by either using modern methods and best practices or adopting cutting-edge technology. I have dwelt a bit on this in the paragraphs above (Lucrative) but will elaborate further. Doubling of income must be solved from 'all' the directions: quantity and quality of produce, price of produce, cost of cultivation, transportation, storage and reduction in wastage (post-harvest losses [PHLs] can be as high as 30%–40% and low-cost, low-tech implements can save a large part of this[6]). Another way of increasing income may simply be to reduce the income of other parts of the value chain, sine qua non. This is one of the most important focus of the book because usage of even the simplest of technologies which are already easily available even in India can address most of the variables which I have mentioned here (lucrative, independent and sustainable). It would be appropriate for me to refer to Ramesh Chand's (member of NITI Aayog) note on this subject published in March 2017.[7] He lists five main points to achieve higher incomes for the farmer: crop choice, higher yield, lower cost, multicropping and

---

[6] Course on 'Global Postharvest Loss Prevention', conducted by the University of Illinois, Urbana-Champaign, as offered on Coursera.
[7] https://niti.gov.in/writereaddata/files/document_publication/DOUBLING%20FARMERS%20INCOME.pdf

higher realizations via better market linkages. For yield, cost and prices, technology use has been brought up as a way to achieve improvements. I suggest a very pervasive use of technology across all aspects.

To sum up the SOLID framework and approach, it primarily focuses on three key aspects of the solution: sustainable, profitable and independent of government or the weather. It is my endeavour to lay down here in this book how technology (again defined very broadly) is the best solution to achieve all these three. In a way, to achieve a profitable, self-sustaining agribusiness, deep and broad usage of technology is crucial and can also be used by the smallest of farmers and even in a gradual manner, that is, by taking small bites rather than a big bang approach.

LIBERALIZATION OF FARMING FROM RULES, REGULATIONS AND RESTRICTIONS

I am conscious of the fact that to build a SOLID farming model and approach, a few key building blocks have to be in place, the most important being unshackling the sector and liberalizing it from the innumerable rules, regulations and restrictions which are currently placed. While there is a valid reason why the restrictions were justified when they were first created (protecting farmers from exploitation, ensuring certain levels of output, preventing hoarding, etc.), many of them have served their purpose and, as a dear friend once said to me, 'every medicine has an expiry date'. It would be unfair to ask the farmers to rise to the occasion with their hands tied. Currently, rules, restrictions or bottlenecks exist on almost every step of the way, from input procurement and price to crop choice, storage, market access and all the way to pricing and even financing. It is imperative that all the nodes in the value chain are opened, allowing farmers to take smarter business decisions based on fundamentals and economics, rather than based on what restrictions allow them to do and where.

I will dwell a little more here on some specifics. India saw its economic liberalization in the early 1990s with reforms and opening of various sectors. It can be argued that this liberalization led to very strong growth for decades. But the agricultural sector was not a part of this. Its time has come now, and we can expect very strong growth now from the agri sector too, if such liberalization takes place. However, it is not simple to apply the same template of economic liberalization to agriculture, as it is an essential commodity and extremely fragmented, with farmers having little bargaining power and with participants who are vulnerable to be exploited. Hence, a reform in this sector must be treated with a different approach and pace. I will outline below a few major areas where this must happen.

1. **Land size:** Small farm holdings on average hamper economics at the farm level as well as investments. Without altering ownership patterns, land aggregation is possible by safer leasing agreements, farming collectives as well as farmer producer organizations (FPOs). There is a lot of scope to clean up the long list of rules around this (also each state has different rules and strictness of implementation) and simplify them in a unified way.

2. **Choice of crop:** This is an indirect problem induced by certain policies like minimum support price (MSP), as a farmer's choice gets driven by crops which have such price support and procurement visibility rather than pure agronomic considerations.

3. **Supply chain and market access:** Many states restrict farmers to sell their produce only in certain markets. Open access to farmers will lead to better price discovery and lower intermediary charges (e.g., electronic national agricultural market [eNAM] and other e-commerce marketplaces like Agribazaar).

4. **Storage:** Farmers are fragmented and have almost no bargaining power when it comes to selling. They have to accept the prevailing prices in the market. If short-term, mini-storage infrastructure can be made available to them in proximity to their farms and at an affordable price, it could give them staying power and prevent them from selling when prices are weak. This can also benefit the government to estimate stock levels if more farmers are able to hold their produce and are required to report it. This is not only important for the farmers, but even the buyers (wholesalers, exporters, etc.), who are the main users of current private storage infrastructure, should report their stocks. This will give the government a complete picture of stocks in the country held by both the Food Corporation of India (FCI) and private parties.

5. **Financing:** Reforms here would be needed in two areas: better and easier financing against stored produce (post-harvest financing) and better access to working capital loans as well as closer monitoring of pre-harvest financing (primarily through Kisan Credit Cards [KCCs]), which currently, in practicality, allows farmers to do unfettered drawdowns with no end-use monitoring.

6. **Input prices:** The government subsidizes fertilizer prices. Farmers tend to use fertilizer mix without very scientific logic or soil test data. Often, the mix is dependent on cheapest fertilizer available and can lead to overuse or underuse of the inputs.

7. **Trade:** Policies and rules around importing and exporting agricultural commodities are governed by the World Trade Organization rules, of which India is a party. But the government has a lot of flexibility in it. In the past, on an ad hoc and tactical basis, the government has banned or allowed imports or exports of commodities based on very short-term needs. While that is the prerogative of the government and is needed, a clearer and liberal

framework would be very useful in allowing farmers to plan their 'business' better, as prices can dramatically change due to such trade rule changes.

While many of the areas mentioned above have seen some action by the government (Agricultural Produce Market Committee [APMC], essential commodities and contract farming), some of the reforms suggested above (MSP imbalance and KCC end-use monitoring) have not been talked about much. I have raised both these issues quite strongly in my first book, *A Wall Street View of Rural India* (June 2020).

LIBERATE THE FARMER BY ALLOWING A FREE ENVIRONMENT

The final piece of the puzzle towards a SOLID agribusiness landscape is how the farmers embrace liberalization, technology, modern methods and best practices to fully maximize their returns. This needs a lot of awareness building and training farmers on the use of hard skills such as technology and machines as well as soft skills of risk-taking and business planning. It also needs a lot of handholding along the way and is not a one-time effort but an ongoing one. Farm advisory services (either by government or private sector or a mix) become a key component here. Higher education on scientific methods will make the farmers progressive and create the perfect cocktail—a sector which is liberalized and farmers who are able and willing to use the benefit of their newfound awareness and progressive nature to embrace change and thrive as they derive the maximum benefits from policy and technology changes.

A NOTE OF CAUTION: AGRITECH ALSO BRINGS WITH IT ITS OWN CHALLENGES

Before I end this chapter, I would however like to highlight a note of caution so that the progress of deploying technology into farming is calibrated and balanced.

1. One aspect of agritech which should not be ignored, especially in lower-middle income countries—where the agriculture sector still provides employment directly or indirectly to 50–60 per cent of the population—is the fact that agritech adoption is bound to reduce manpower needs on the farm, whether it is for pre-sowing activity, harvesting and post-harvesting or sorting and packing activity. If technology was adopted at all steps of the value chain, it could dramatically reduce farm labour requirement. For example, even weed cleaning can now be done by machines, whereas most farms in lower-middle income countries still use farm labour to remove weeds manually. As has been seen in the developed world over the decades, modernization and industrialization of farming have released a lot of resources for use in the industry and urban economy. The USA barely has 2–3 per cent of its workforce employed in agriculture. That is not one of the outcomes of technology which lower-middle income countries like India can ignore. On the one hand, there is need to retain farmers on the farm and stop them from leaving the farms, and to adopt modern methods and technology to increase production and profitability. But on the other hand, if that very process is going to free up large amounts of rural farm labour, it will open another problem of absorbing them into the urban workforce. Moreover, as adoption of agritech promises to reduce the drudgery involved in farming activities, it will attract more youth to stay back and re-engage in family farming businesses, thereby further reducing the need of external farm labourers.

2. The second aspect to balance is the rural digital divide.[8] We have to understand this in three or four different

---

[8] World Economic Forum, *Innovation with a Purpose: The Role of Technology Innovation in Accelerating Food Systems Transformation* (2018), http://www3.weforum.org/docs/WEF_Innovation_with_a_Purpose_VF-reduced.pdf

ways. Large tech platform companies will have access and control over a lot of data, as it gets concentrated in the hands of a few. Many agribusinesses are also backward or forward integrating and gaining control of a larger piece of the pie. Within the farming community itself, the large, rich and educated farmers will have more access than the others. Another slice of this is the women in farming, who may not enjoy equal access to technology or may be less skilled at using it. This creates the risk with which agritech and its benefits further polarize farmers and increase the rural divide, rather than reducing it. Another aspect of this is that given the differences in affordability and adaptability, technology will get adopted at different paces at different parts of the value chain. We could see more adoption downstream than mid-stream and the least upstream. This uneven adoption across the value chain will also create imbalances and make the profit pool shift in undesirable ways. To reduce these, proper education and training are key as well as basic telecom infrastructure to ensure a balanced adoption.

From an Indian context, the governments must hence focus on maximizing the positive and minimizing the negative impacts.

With this framework in mind, we will tackle each of the six parts of the SOLID approach and look at each component (crop selection, multicropping, cost efficiencies, yield, variety and price realization) of a farmer's earning so that it can be doubled with the smart use of technology. Many of the chapters and sections are organized in this manner to continue with this flow of our arguments.

CHAPTER 2

BEATING THE SIZE PROBLEM

Ground-up Story: Small Can Be Beautiful

'It's called *small but smart*,' he said to me as he tried to tell me that he understood my point.

This was the head of a Krishi Vigyan Kendra (KVK) in Bihar, whom I was speaking with. Our discussion had veered towards how to accelerate the change in behaviour of small farmers but at a large scale. I used the word 'success stories', and he immediately stopped me. He told me that he agreed with the view that it is critical to share success stories, but there is no point in talking about the large farmers. No one will get inspired with hearing only those stories. I asked him about KVK's work with regard to small farmers. This really piqued his interest and a 30-minute conversation turned into a 90-minute discussion. He told me about the 'exposure visits' which are basically focusing on the small farmers who are willing to try new things, and once they achieve some progress and outcomes, they take large groups of farmers to showcase what success they have had. That is when he told me about a report that he and his agricultural university (AU) had published a few years ago. It was a compilation of several similar case studies called 'Small but Smart Farmer'. I was really impressed, so I had to ask him: 'You seem to have ticked all the boxes and showed me that all the right things are being done then why is it that things are not improving?'

He was a little taken aback at the blatant question, but he got the drift. With a lot of seriousness in his voice, he said, '*Janaab,* bad news spreads fast in these areas, good news stays hidden.' I couldn't agree more.

This story foretells the gist of the chapter—how small farmers can also thrive if they learn and adopt the right things and get good handholding and advise along the way.

Any discussion, article or even a book on Indian agriculture and its characteristics tends to start with the fact that the average Indian farm holding is very small. It is just about 2.5 acres. The same in the USA, for example, is over 400 acres and in Australia is a whopping 11,000 acres.[1] What is more interesting is that the blame for almost all the problems, weaknesses and challenges faced by the Indian farmer and agriculture is squarely placed on this small size. I quote from an old interview by the then NABARD chairman, 'The agriculture sector in the country is under stress. For, the land holdings are constantly decreasing. This has resulted in discouraging farmers to invest in the field because of small land at their disposal.'[2] I will share another quote from an article by Subanandhini D. written in December 2020[3]: 'Even though India stands second in terms of production of rice and wheat, in terms of productivity it ranks 52 and 38 respectively. The main reason behind this is the small landholding which leads to less mechanization....' And this quote by A. S. Mittal, the vice chairman of the Punjab State Planning Board, does not mince any words, 'In farming, size matters ... on an average,

[1] https://www.abs.gov.au/AUSSTATS/abs@.nsf/Lookup/7121.0Main+Features12015-16
[2] https://www.business-standard.com/article/economy-policy/solution-to-indian-agriculture-is-aggregation-dr-prakash-bakshi-113090600679_1.html
[3] https://diplomatist.com/2020/12/03/the-future-of-smallholder-farming-in-india/

smaller farmers lose money as their household costs are higher than their earnings....'[4]

This is not untrue. A larger size of farm holding does lend itself to several benefits which can help improve the income of the farmer. While we will talk a lot about that in this chapter, I want to draw the reader's attention to a little different view here.

How can we live with our small and marginal farms (defined by the government as anything less than 2.5 acres) and make the most of them? I look at this issue in two ways. First, that this polarization is not unique to India. World over, whether it is the USA or Italy, only a fraction of the farms are really large, and the bulk of them are small. This is in the nature of farming because farms originally have been family owned and hence by definition very fragmented and small. So if it is a global phenomenon and small farms still exist elsewhere, there is no need for such a defeatist approach in India, as if there was nothing a small holder farmer could do.

And second, that this need not mean that small farms have to be unviable. The fact is that this small absolute size is embedded and cannot be wished away so easily. Of the about 150 m farm holdings in India, 86 per cent are of less than 2.5 acres. And only 0.56 per cent are of more than 25 acres.[5] Hence, we must embrace what we have and find solutions to make the most of it. Often, the block is only in the mind, and even at a small unit level, better practices can be adopted. It is again, here, that technology comes to the rescue because it offers multiple ways to improve overall earning even with small holdings. Precision farming, for example, does not

---
[4] https://www.hindustantimes.com/opinion/farm-to-factory-small-farmersneed-second-source-of-income/story-sy9JxnUHcP0kMmhCUMw6dP.html
[5] https://www.insightsonindia.com/2020/07/10/the-average-size-of-holdings-has-shown-a-steady-declining-trend-over-the-last-three-decades-what-are-the-challenges-faced-by-farmers-due-to-fragmentation-of-land-what-needs-to-be-done-in-this-regard/

need a large farm size. Indeed, even a small farmer can be a beneficiary of the agritech revolution and modern methods that this book talks about.

INHERENT DICHOTOMY OF INDIAN FARMS: POLARIZED SCALE AND ECONOMICS

When there is so much polarization in size, it usually also comes with an extreme or maybe even wider polarization in economics of the two farms. So the inequality in rural India is already heightened. The small and marginal farmers are extremely poor, while the upper half per cent are probably wealthier than many urban businessmen, further helped by the fact that agricultural income in India is tax free, and even the very large farmers are eligible for most of the subsidies and grants.

WEAKEST LINK LEFT OUT

Another very pertinent point is that of the rural digital divide. Much has been said about the small and marginal farmers being left out of coverage and the benefits of agritech and hence being the weakest link. Even if there is technology which can help small farmers, they are the least likely to know of it, be able to afford it or adopt it, implying that small size also brings with it disadvantages of ability and affordability. I have referred to the report by the World Economic Forum (WEF) on the downside of agritech in Chapter 1 (note 8) which also highlights this.

THREE WAYS BY WHICH EVEN SMALL FARMS CAN THRIVE AND FLOURISH

In this chapter, I focus on outlining the three ways in which, I believe, even small farmers can thrive and flourish. I will explain each one in detail below. In Box 2.1 I have also tried to clarify differences between some of these ways that may sound similar but are not.

Box 2.1. Farm Collectives: Is It Different from Land Aggregation, Cooperatives and FPOs?

Anyone reading about the various ways of getting farmers together is bound to get confused between a cooperative, an FPO, a farmer producer company (FPC), collective farming (CF) and land leasing. A cooperative is a group of farmers usually growing the same commodity coming together (e.g., sugar, milk and strawberries). An FPO is a cooperative without the focus on a single crop. An FPC is an FPO which is incorporated as a corporate entity, thus giving each member one vote and maintaining a democratic ownership and control of large and small farmers and is free to include many commodities without any restriction. It also comes with all the other benefits of a limited liability company and a corporate structure for governance. However, a farm collective or CF (also known sometimes as communal farming) is slightly different. It can be a part of an FPC's activities too but has not yet been the case. The main differentiation is that in a CF, the actual cultivation activity itself is done collectively. Cropping and other decisions on inputs, farming process and marketing are all undertaken as one unit. Proceeds are distributed among the members according to their cultivated land share in the pool. Most people involved with FPOs/FPCs feel that this pooled cultivation is more difficult to achieve due to heterogenous inputs used and maybe even output as well as more personal habits and customs. Some have felt that due to missing land entitlements, land pooling has not been possible in India. Hence, although FPOs and FPCs engage in a lot of collective operations related to farming, the actual farms and farming itself are not pooled at all. Some private and new farmers (urban background) have started CFs in several parts of the country, but the members are mostly new farmers and not traditional ones. The CF concept is a communist concept practised in China, the Soviet, Vietnam, etc., where the land was pooled together to achieve economies of scale. There is an example in Tamil Nadu state in India

(continued)

(continued)

> where about 35 women have come together, leased in land and shared the actual farming work and produce. On the other hand, almost all the FPOs (even large, successful ones like Sahyadri Farms in Nashik) or start-ups like Kamatan in Bengaluru focus on working with farmers or other FPOs in procurement, marketing and some advisory. Without going into the 'title' part of this debate or the communist/socialist aspect of land owned by the state, I just want to highlight that the cooperation seen in a cooperative and collaboration seen in an FPO/FPC should be taken a step further to extend that to actual cultivation too, so that true benefits of scale, not only of purchasing and selling but also of on-farm productivity, can also be had as well as that of co-investment into machines and other infrastructure (storage, greenhouses and post-harvest implements), which a single farmer cannot afford to buy or even rent.

Make the Most of It

This first approach focuses on looking inward and making the most of what one has. If a farmer just has a 2-acre plot and has no other option but to run it on their own, they can still do it profitably. There are several ways of doing it, but instead of making it too prescriptive, I will attempt to give a broad flavour of the methods we are talking about, also because I revisit this subtopic in more detail in the book later.

1. **Number and choice of crops:** This refers to the best practices and modern methods applied in choosing the crops based on agronomics (soil, weather and water) and yield, demand, price, acreage, etc., so that you maximize your profit per acre. As highlighted by Ramesh Chand (Chapter 1, footnote 7), the revenue per hectare differs widely based on what is grown, and a farmer can earn as high as ₹1.4 lakh from horticulture or high-value crops or as low as ₹27,000 from growing pulses. Second, multicropping and intercropping

can be adopted, which will allow the farmer to enjoy two–three crops a year. This can increase the total volume of crop you are producing manifold as well as diversify the risk (e.g., one crop with no intercropping vs three crops with intercropping). In India, on average, as per Mr Chand's report, only 39 per cent of cultivated land is used for 2 or more crops. In most states, it's only 25 per cent. Even while sticking to the same crop (e.g., an apple orchard) just experimenting with better varieties, the yield per acre can go up significantly. There are dozens of examples in Himachal Pradesh where young engineering graduates not finding jobs returned to family orchards, brought in new varieties of apples from Europe which required one-fourth the land area and could flower and produce in just two years (refer to box 'The Himachal Model' in Chapter 4).

2. **Input optimizing:** A farmer can reduce their costs by using less inputs (precision and intensive farming) or buying them cheaper (online marketplaces) or using more recycled natural organic material (zero-cost natural farming [ZNCF]). They can also reduce other inputs like water (rainwater harvesting, automated drip irrigation, weather info and sensors) or electricity (solar powered) at the farm and even optimize nutrient and pesticide usage by soil testing and using precision farming sensors as well as efficient spraying gadgets.

3. **Optimizing realization:** By either delaying sale (holding on to it in a warehouse) or selling in marketplaces (rather than designated *mandis*), they can improve realization. Or even by tying up with large direct buyers/contract farming, they can reduce commissions paid to the middlemen.

4. **Preventing losses:** Another very important way to improve income is to just reduce losses. There are several reasons a farmer experiences loss of produce. It could be pests or animals which devour the crop (monkeys and wild pigs) or it could be winter frost. Simple solutions for

this are available (fences, nets, advance weather or pest warning systems). A little upfront cost but savings will be perennial. Moreover, local governments in many states give huge grants to purchase or install such apparatus. There are other losses from not storing produce properly or not drying it and during harvesting itself or during threshing. Use of machines can reduce some of these losses materially ('Global Postharvest Loss Prevention' course by the University of Illinois Urbana-Champaign).

Land Aggregation: The Underappreciated Solution

The second way in which a small farmer can still do well is to, well, not remain a small farmer, that is, to join hands with other farmers and run a big farm collectively with all its attendant benefits or lease farmland from others. Land aggregation is often misunderstood and confused with contract farming. Here, I refer to farmers themselves getting into a collective or leasing in. The 2020 reforms passed by the government, for example, did not touch upon this but instead addressed the contract farming rules, which some thought was the same thing. Land lease is a state subject and governed by different laws across states which provide different levels of protection to the landlord and the tenant. Hence, adoption of this mechanism has been poor. On paper it is allowed in many states and the Central government has also passed a model law on this. It is also being practised in some states. But still it's far from becoming a normal way of doing things. Only about 14 per cent of arable land in India is reported as under tenancy as I outline later. There is definite scope for widening its adoption nationwide by passing laws where none exist, simplifying laws where they are complex and ensuring safeguards where there are loopholes.

It is worthwhile here to go a bit into history. In British India, the feudal system was in prevalence and *zamindari* was widely present. Rich landlords extracted high sums of money from poor cultivators who tilled their land for them. Post Independence, to stem this, governments across the country tried to distribute this land to the tillers. And to achieve that, many ended up even banning tenancy altogether. Even states which allowed it capped the rent to 20–25 per cent of the produce value. This was way below the market rates prevalent then. What followed was hence informal, verbal arrangements in such states. Now, with ever-dropping size of average holdings, there is a need to enable tenancy again but with strong legal framework so that both the landlord and the tenant enjoy benefits in a fair manner and have security of land ownership or tenure of lease. Arvind Panagariya, the ex-head of NITI Aayog, has written an informative article on this, which I will refer to here and reproduce some of the data mentioned in it in Table 2.1.[6]

No.	State	Lease Law Status	Comments
1	Telangana	Banned	Exceptions on defence, widows, disabled people
2	Bihar	Banned	Exceptions on defence, widows, disabled people
3	Karnataka	Banned	Exceptions on defence, widows, disabled people
4	Madhya Pradesh	Allowed	Exceptions on defence, widows, disabled people/liberalized in 2017
5	Uttar Pradesh	Allowed	Exceptions on defence, widows, disabled people/modified since 2017
6	Kerala	Banned	Recently allowed self-help groups (SHGs) to lease in
7	Punjab	Allowed	Tenant has right to buy after some years
8	Haryana	Allowed	Tenant has right to buy after some years

(continued)

---

[6] https://niti.gov.in/writereaddata/files/document_publication/NITIBlog2_VC.pdf

(continued)

No.	State	Lease Law Status	Comments
9	Gujarat	Allowed	Tenant has right to buy after some years
10	Maharashtra	Allowed	Tenant has right to buy after some years
11	Assam	Allowed	Tenant has right to buy after some years
12	Andhra Pradesh	Liberally allowed	Fully liberalized
13	Tamil Nadu	Liberally allowed	No sharecropping allowed
14	Rajasthan	Liberally allowed	No sharecropping allowed
15	West Bengal	Liberally allowed	Only sharecropping allowed (where crop share is paid as rent)
16	Uttarakhand	Allowed	Allowed since modifications made in 2017

Table 2.1. Summary of State-wise Land Lease Laws in India

Source: https://niti.gov.in/writereaddata/files/document_publication/NITI Blog2_VC.pdf

The benefits to the tenant are innumerable. The farmer has visibility on their tenure of tenancy and can invest money on cultivation, can borrow for such activities and can get crop insurance payouts, which currently do not go to a tenant. From the landlord perspective, the biggest risk is losing their land; hence, if they have clear indefeasible title (through digital land records), they will also feel secure in getting into these contracts. If digital land records are not available (only Karnataka has it), then registration of such contracts can be done at panchayat level, rather than revenue department level, to remove or reduce their risk of losing their land if a policy change were to go after such contracts and redistribute land to such farmers. The benefits to the government are also many. It can stop the product-based subsidy system used in fertilizers, for example, and start a direct benefit transfer (DBT)-based more efficient system. Second, various studies have shown that about 25 m hectares of arable land (total base of ~150 m) is lying fallow because of such hurdles where the landowner is not keen to rent it out.

NITI Aayog had prepared a model lease agreement in 2016, which could be the basis for states adopting this. In 2017, it shared it with the states and two or three of them have since modified their laws accordingly. If the lease term and rent are left to the participants to decide and clear dispute resolution responsibility and timeframes are fixed, it should be palatable and acceptable.

In spite of this, however, about 12–14 per cent (as per NABARD All India Rural Financial Inclusion Survey 2016–17)[7] of Indian agricultural households leased in farmland. Figures for 2012–2013 from this report indicate that the percentage of tenant holding was about 14 per cent of arable land in India. Not a small number, but it can become much bigger and improve overall yields and incomes for the entire ecosystem. The caveat here is that the 12–14 per cent is the *reported* number, while majority of such arrangements are still verbal and not registered anywhere, which means that the actual number is *much* higher. In fact, almost 3 in 10 farmers I spoke to have leased in some land and almost *all* of them have done it on a verbal basis except one farmer in Karnataka. Official agreements will make it more palatable to landlords to rent out. In fact, as the need to target the youth into agriculture rises, such legal frameworks will be of immense help in allowing them to lease and start farming activity.

FPOs: Creating Benefits of Scale for the Small Farmer

The third and another very important solution to the small holding problem of Indian agriculture is the FPOs. It is the

---

[7] https://www.financialexpress.com/opinion/land-leasing-where-are-the-tenancy-reforms/1985318/

coming together of a farmer community or cluster with common objectives, goals, problems and challenges, which uses the benefits of size to improve farming efficiency—whether it is procurement, sale, raising finance, adopting new practices or crops. FPOs have been around for many years in India. By FY2019, there were about 10,000 of them. The government announced in their Union budget that year that they intended to increase this number to 20,000 in 2–3 years. The objective was the same: to ensure that the small farmer is not left out from the agriculture reforms and opportunities, and benefits of all policy moves and the opportunity trickle down to the lowest common denominator, thus making them run a viable operation.

Like all good things though, FPOs have had their own set of problems. The main one being the lack of initiative by fellow farmers to take leadership and get the community together. Second, even once you have a leader, it is difficult to convince farmers to join in because they don't see the benefit or are sceptical about it due to past experience or generally being suspect about any change. Third, many existing FPOs have not had too much success to showcase it around (particularly the ones driven top-down or Small Farmers' Agri-Business Consortium [SFAC]-supported ones) because either they have not been able to flourish within the fairly tight constraints, budgets and timelines of the FPO rules (set by SFAC) or big benefits have not come through either in raising finance (particularly) or they are abandoned by the CEOs once the two-year period of grant is over (₹5 lakh per year).

I will outline the key working rules around FPOs and highlight what changes are underway already. I continue to feel that building awareness and trust is probably the biggest problem, followed by ability to attract, train and retain CEOs as well as a competent and motivated board of directors (BODs) to run the FPOs. Finally, broadcasting success stories to build confidence will go a long way.

Going a little deeper here, I would like to sum up the history of FPOs in India, what problems they face and what solutions are needed. FPOs have been there since the early 2000s and are not new in concept. In fact, in 2002, the Government of India (GoI) amended the Companies Act and introduced the FPC as a special entity on the recommendations of Y. K. Alagh Committee (2001). That year itself, about 500 FPCs were registered and now there are a total of about 7,000+ such companies.[8] Some of them are very large, pan-India multi-state organizations, with nearly 150,000 members, while some are very niche, limiting themselves to few hundred farmers within only 1 village. A 2018 report by MANAGE (National Institute of Agricultural Extension Management) has highlighted a lot of the benefits of FPOs, along with several success stories.[9] However, for a country of 150 million farmers, the penetration is still extremely low.

The role that cooperation between farmers can play—within any structure—is mainly one of scale and collective bargaining in buying inputs at lower prices and in selling their produce to wholesale or end customers at higher prices, due to larger collective volumes being transacted. Another big help is training on technology, best practices and modern methods. Higher value addition through processing and brand building is perhaps a more advanced activity but being followed by several FPOs. Fundraising (pre-harvest and post-harvest) is another benefit. And these are well known and understood. What is probably less appreciated or explored yet is how this same scale can be used *on the farm* itself in terms of more mechanization and technology used in cultivation itself, things which were not viable with a small farm but become viable with a larger farm size. This does presuppose contiguous

---

[8] https://thewire.in/economy/nobody-knows-how-many-farmer-producer-companies-there-are-in-india
[9] https://www.manage.gov.in/publications/edigest/jun2018.pdf

landholdings of members at times. But that itself can become the selling point to attract neighbouring farmland owners to join hands. And, in fact, this was at the very heart of the government initiative called One District One Product—basically a cluster approach. I talk about this in another chapter too, where I highlight global experiences on this and how CF and cluster approach can be very value-enhancing for farmers. There are already several success stories across states such as Uttarakhand, Rajasthan, Gujarat, Maharashtra, Karnataka, Odisha and West Bengal.[10] Companies such as Masuta, VAPCOL, Navjyoti, VGAI (Narayangaon), Raitha Mithra, Kamaraj Progressive FPC and Ram Rahim have been in operation for years and are clear success stories with tangible benefits to their members. But it appears that the progress of this wave has stalled. Although in FY2019 and FY2020, the government accelerated its focus on this area by granting a tax holiday, matching equity contribution, loan guarantee and aggressive targets to increase the number of FPOs.[11]

Hence, on digging deeper, I summarize a few key reasons for it and update with some recent progress made by the government and private sector, and also provide my own solutions to further accelerate this.

1. **Talent:** The vast scope of an FPO (production to marketing to finance to technology) needs a lot of senior talent. To attract and retain such talent, the FPO will have to pay market-linked compensation. Current rules have restrictions on maximum salary payable to an FPO CEO, if supported by SFAC. In the initial years, the governing bodies of NABARD and SFAC had run very intense CEO and board member training programmes. A lot of those

---

[10] https://yourstory.com/2019/03/farmer-producer-organisations-fpo-agritech-4l6kpppbt4/amp

[11] https://www.drishtiias.com/daily-updates/daily-news-editorials/farmers-producer-organisation

highly trained cohort are no longer in the system, and now good talent is difficult to find. Farmers are keen to get together and take up collective operations and activities but lack the leadership. Training of CEOs and BODs used to be taken up very stringently in the early years of the FPOs. Now that is hardly being done, resulting in lack of talent to run these companies. It is also not fully fair to expect the government to also provide the talent to run these FPOs. It is now for the private sector and social entrepreneurs to rise to the occasion and accelerate this.

2. **Finance:** FPOs face great difficulty in accessing finance on their own. In such cases, they should focus only on advice to help each member raise loans rather than high capex activities. But to raise finance for itself, it needs to be enabled via a larger capital base, marginable assets and more flexible banks, as they will need grants and financial assistance to set up infrastructure like custom hiring centres (CHCs) or warehouses.

3. **Focus:** FPOs have mainly focused on procurement, market linkages and some processing/branding. One key benefit of aggregation is CF, which we have not seen much evidence of yet. FPOs/FPCs have been known to benefit their members by ₹8,000–₹10,000 per year per member. Some case studies have shown benefits of 8–10 per cent in costs or 10–15 per cent in prices. This is still a very small amount. The big impact hence will be of collectives where yields and costs can have a much bigger impact. Another activity under focus is of advisory on cultivation methods. There are few examples of that (new methods of growing saplings in greenhouses, increasing planting distance, allowing intercropping and multicropping); these can also have very large impact on farmer incomes.

4. **Structure:** Only producer farmers can be members, and only members can contribute to equity capital. So a private sector entrepreneur who is not a farmer himself

will not be able to contribute. The cap of 1,000 farmers (now reduced to 500 only) is a problem because while targets of 10,000 can be achieved, the scale benefits with just 1,000 farmers will not come through.

5. **Short duration of support:** An important issue highlighted to me in all my FPO interactions was that the support of ₹5 lakh per year given for just two years is too short. They need two more years. Getting 1,000 farmers joined up via farmer interest groups (FIGs) and doing the legal incorporation work as appointment of the board, etc., itself takes more than 1 year. That barely leaves any time to the entity to start any fruitful work.

6. **Market challenges:** Creating market linkages even after forward integration into value added products is very difficult and takes a long time to study the market and come up with a differentiating brand or product.

7. **All FPOs are not the same:** Privately promoted FPOs (no SFAC grant) or bottoms-up promoted FPOs (by the farmer organically) are the ones which are really doing well, while the others are struggling. SFAC-supported FPOs face restrictions, and those which are pushed down from the top lack motivation. Top-down means that the board and CEO are appointed before even getting in the members. This should be a totally bottoms-up process. It is such 'top-down' FPOs which have usually failed to achieve much success and which sign up farmers who do it more as an obligation or because a senior local 'leader' is asking for it.

8. **Scepticism—Changes in FPOs:** One of the reasons I noted for farmers being vary of FPOs is their unpleasant past experience. There have been farmer cooperatives in the past as well as SHGs, Kisan Clubs and FIGs. They were converted from one form to another many times before too. Again, they have been converted into FPOs, and many are again shutting down or stuck due to lack

of funds or managers. Farmers, hence, feel that they are not consulted before new programmes are launched. One FPO CEO told me that all this start–stop does a lot of emotional damage to the farmer. It is clear that we need one unified umbrella body, speaking one language, giving out a longer-term clear glide path, so that this scepticism can also be reduced over time.

To sum it up, having FPOs is a very powerful way to alleviate the small farmer woes and allow them to also thrive and flourish. FPOs have existed for last 20 years and have many success stories too. But the spread has been slow although accelerating in the last three years. FPOs have some bottlenecks mainly of fundraising. I feel that less focus should be on asset-heavy activity and more on advisory and farming techniques and CF, rather than processing food. Fundraising even for investments should be done from within. That way, the FPO will not need much capital and will have a larger feeling of ownership among farmers.

Overall, this chapter concludes with three key messages: Small size of farm holdings in India is a problem, but farmers can still thrive by being smarter and more efficient in their small farms and embracing technology, land aggregation through land lease agreements and via FPOs and CF.

PART

THE WHO AND HOW OF FARMING

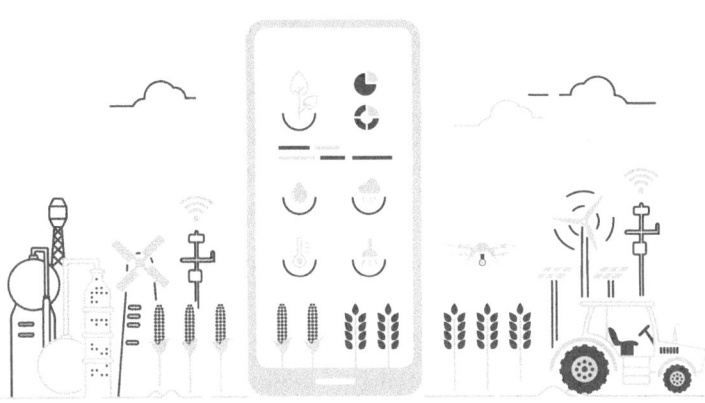

CHAPTER 3

WHO WILL RUN THE FARMS?

Ground-up Story: All Hands on Deck—An Uncommon Feature

I had just arrived at Theog—a remote town about 100 km away from Shimla—on a chilly December afternoon. It had been a great four-hour drive up the mountains from the Chandigarh airport, and I couldn't wait to meet up with a bunch of farmers who were scheduled to meet me at a local tea shop. Durga Das was the senior-most among them and doing most of the talking. We met and settled down with hot cups of tea. There were three of them between their early 30s to late 40s. All of them were still dressed in their work clothes, which irked my curiosity, as it was quite late in the day and was not even sowing or harvesting season. I learnt that even in the deep winter, when their apple harvest was months away, they had to take care of the trees and protect their roots and branches from the wind, snow and pests. They had to manually tie them up, so they don't sway too much and lose their branches.

The question on top of my mind was about their family farming history, with regard to their cultivation, the status of the farm economics, and their future aspirations and the changes they desire in their everyday routine.

Here's what I learnt. The farmers basically owned apple orchards high up in the mountains and grew some vegetables in the lower areas and during the lean periods. It was a family of three sons, their mother, wives and children. And all eight of them were actively engaged in running and tending to their farm and farm animals, even their old mother, wives and young sons. This was very heartening to hear but also very surprising. Here was a family where all the three generations were involved in farming and were proud and happy about it. It was so different from what I had come to get used to over a decade of my rural travels.

When I probed further, I was told that even their mother, to that day, whenever needed would go into orchards and tend to the trees, clearing them of shrubs and weeds as well as checking them to see whether they 'looked' healthy or not. Yes indeed, just by looking at them! It was the responsibility of the women of the house to take care of the farm animals, not because they could not afford some farm hands but because the family believed in everyone being involved and doing their bit. Lastly, their sons showed interest voluntarily and kept offering their help whenever they had time to do odd jobs around the farm. Indeed, a fairy tale farming family! If only we had more of such....

The next day I met Rajendra, another apple farmer, who was himself a second-generation farmer, and probed further on the agritech aspects. He told me, to my surprise, that the local government agriculture wing conducted training and advisory sessions for farmers every six months. And he said that he diligently participated in those. There, they learnt new scientific methods and experiences of other farmers. He found it useful, but I sensed a feeling that there was lack of follow-through after attending those sessions, and there were not many like him who attended these. Most of them shrugged it off saying that it won't work for them even if on paper it sounds good. He also mentioned to me a private individual who had done his own experiments and was growing a much higher number of apple trees in a small farm and running the operation at a very low cost. He also holds 'workshops' for farmers on a non-profit basis—to educate them. Usually, I was told that the distance between 2 apple trees needs to be about 8–10 feet. In the olden day, people used to plant these even further apart. But this individual had experimented with much lesser distance—about 4–6 feet and yet managing a good yield and quality. Before I signed off, he also mentioned that in his family of five brothers, they grew apples, plums, cauliflowers, almonds, pears, beans and peas. His 18-year-old son was studying but taking a lot of interest in farming. And finally, that they didn't use tractors (still using oxen) but did use machines for grading their harvest, though not yet for packing or plucking their produce!

From the two meetings, I realized how the whole family is involved in farming and that they are forward thinking and curious to learn. Such an attitude is crucial to keep the youth plugged in.

As of 2016, the average age of the Indian farmer was about 50 years.[1] Hence, it is safe to say that after working for 10–15 years, the average farmer will retire from active farming life. With high rates of migration from villages to cities, most of the rural youth has not worked on a farm for most of their lives, having left the village for a better working life in the cities. These youngsters come back reluctantly only when they must. Hence, it won't be any surprise if a farmer's third generation (his grandchildren) is even less interested in farming and is pursuing education with great enthusiasm and positivity to make careers in the mainstream economy. In my previous book *A Wall Street View of Rural India* (2020), I have called this phenomenon the grain drain. Now as even families become supportive of this transitioning of family occupation, it begets the question: Who will then run the farms?

---

[1] https://www.downtoearth.org.in/blog/agriculture/farmers-ageing-new-generation-disinterested-who-will-grow-our-food--65800

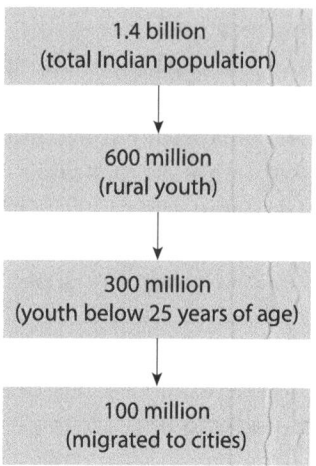

Figure 3.1. The Math behind the Grain Drain

It is easy to do the math and realize that we are talking of just 10–15 years in which this question must not only be answered but also implemented and executed. In fact, a World Bank study projects that only 25.7 per cent of Indian workforce would be involved in agriculture in 2050 vs 58.2 per cent in 2001.[2] And therein lies the urgency with which not just the government but all stakeholders—farmers themselves and entrepreneurs—must address this head on. Throughout this book, I have made the conscious effort to lay down the 'problem' as one owned by farmers themselves and not only something that only the 'government' has to do. The earlier the farmers wean themselves away from the government and create a self-sustaining business model out of their farming activities, the better they would thrive.

Figure 3.1 highlights the math around this and the need and urgency to address this.

---

[2] https://pib.gov.in/Pressreleaseshare.aspx?PRID=1518097

UNDERSTANDING THE CAUSES OF THE GRAIN DRAIN

The reasons we see the younger generation wanting to leave farms are primarily (a) too much hard work, (b) too less visibility, (c) not a path to riches, (d) social stigma, (e) fragmented land, (f) family already disengaged from agriculture, (g) too much risk aversion and (h) lack of farming knowledge. I will explain each of these—even if briefly—because this is so fundamental to the problem and the solution.

Too Much Hard Work

World over, agriculture is seen as hard manual work on the farms in treacherous weather. This is more so in India, where it is seen as drudgery, and a lot of physical labour is involved. Everyone wants to move to a better quality of life, and hence people move towards an easier lifestyle where they want to use their mind and not just do physical work. Given the fact that mechanization is low in India (use of tractors or other farm equipment; 45% in India vs 75% in Brazil),[3] more work is done manually by the farmer and their labourers, whether it is sowing, harvesting, ploughing the field, removing weeds, etc.

Uncertainty of Produce

About 50 per cent of India's arable land is under irrigation, and even that is skewed towards a few states. Hence, the dependence of the farmer on a good amount of rainfall is very high in most parts of the country. This makes their basic economics very unpredictable. Second, the government support provided through MSP and procurement for its public distribution system (PDS)—the price and quantity and even the crops which are purchased under this—keep changing

---

[3] https://www.mordorintelligence.com/industry-reports/tractors-market

frequently. Finally, information on what other farmers are growing and acreage under various crops for the previous season or the oncoming season is all scarce. On top of this, pest attacks or sudden weather changes (unseasonal rain or a frost attack) happen often. Hence, all these reduce the visibility a farmer has on their income in a particular season as they enter the production cycle.

Fragmented Land

It is a well-known fact that the average farm size in India is about 1 hectare (less than 2.5 acres), and 86 per cent of farmers in India are classified as small or marginal. A small farm reduces the economies of scale (getting lower price for inputs and higher for the output is difficult) and makes the inherent viability quite lacklustre. This adds to the lack of appeal of farming activity for the younger generations.

Family Already Disengaged

Because of many of the above problems (or all of them), many farming families have already disengaged from full-time farming. This is either by renting out their farms to other informal aggregators or by employing labourers and managers, thus keeping their involvement to the bare minimum. In my travels and meetings, I have found a much larger cohort of such farmers than I was happy to. Given this disengagement, it is difficult to then expect the younger generations to find or rediscover the interest in farming.

Lack of Farming Knowledge

This is a fallout of the above, in some sense. By this, I mean traditional knowledge as well as knowledge of modern methods. Not having been working on the farm themselves, the young farmer has never learnt the basic skills and knowledge about farming to start with. In addition, the amount of progress made globally on farming practices is totally lost on them. So they tend to not have much interest.

Too Much Risk Aversion

I strongly feel that this is the least discussed aspect. Over the years, farmers have gotten used to more support from the government, and this has numbed their ability to take risk in their 'business' of farming. It has reached a point where everyone is growing the same crops and realizing lower prices and making less money—a vicious cycle to say the least. This point is closely connected with all the above points as well and also a reason why the youth is quitting farming.

Not a Path to Riches

This is really the core of the problem. Even if the farmer was to deal with the above issues, they do not end up making enough money to sustain their family—basically, all the pain for hardly any gains. Farming is in fact seen as a subsistence activity not only in India but elsewhere too (at least in the past). After factoring in the support prices and various subsidies given by the government, the average income of a farmer in India is about ₹8,931 per month only (NABARD, FY2017). The NSSO estimates it to have touched about ₹10,000 by FY2019.[4] That's less than $130 per month. Now that's hardly something the younger generation wants to hold their breath for!

---

[4] https://www.newindianexpress.com/nation/2020/dec/28/farmers-income-rose-only-by-rs-2505-between-2012-13-and-2016-17-data-2242031.html

Social Stigma vs Pride

This brings me to a softer issue. Even if the farmer and their family surmount all the above problems and are making reasonable money, who wants to be known as a farmer? Is it cool? Would you put it on your Instagram or even LinkedIn profile? You will think many times before you do that. So yes, there is this big social stigma of being seen as a farmer. A farmer in Gujarat recently told me that it would be difficult for a farmer to find a good bride, even if he was earning much more in farming vs a government job. So the younger generation is running in the opposite direction pushed by such social consciousness. In fact, we need to turn this on its head—from stigma to pride in running your farm—and give it the cool factor!

Now that we have understood the multitude of reasons of the grain drain, let's look at what can be done to stem this and even to reverse it.

INDIA IS NOT ALONE IN THIS!

Before we look at some ways to stop this, it is worthwhile to know that many of these dynamics and challenges exist world over, even if in varying degrees. Almost 90 per cent of all farms worldwide are managed by a family or an individual. Only 2 per cent of farms in the world can be defined as large, organized farming businesses. These farms, on the other hand, occupy 70 per cent of the global used agricultural acreage, whereas 72 per cent of farms of less than a hectare occupy just some 8 per cent of agricultural land. Farming has been a very tough activity across history and across the world. The phenomenon of youth leaving farming is being experienced worldwide too, although it may be starker in India, given the low levels of mechanization and smaller landholdings vs world averages. The average age of a US farmer is also approaching 60. How many will stay as family farms? When the existing farmer retires, what happens to those farms? These are questions being asked worldwide even today.

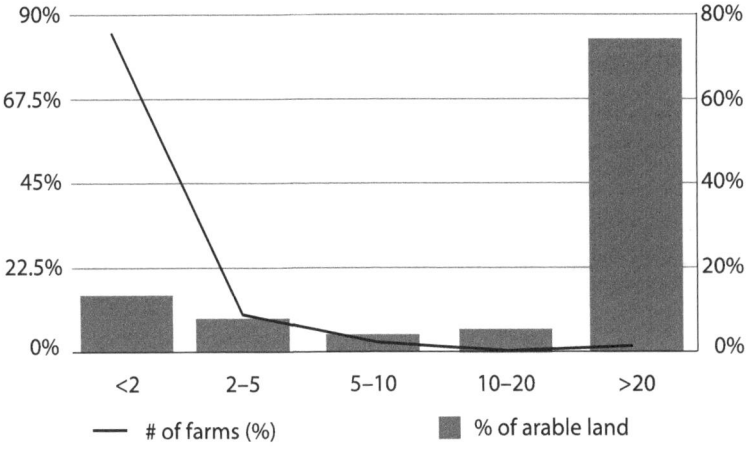

Figure 3.2. Global Distribution of Farm Holdings

Figure 3.2[5] based on a study using FAO data till 2013 sums it up very well.

I mention this to alert the reader to the fact that at some point, if not concurrently, many countries in the world, including the developed ones, are facing similar problems to some degree or other. Hence, it is not unique to India but that also means that we should all be open to and seek out global experience and precedents on how the various stakeholders have reacted and solved or managed this challenge. In fact, areas like agritech, which are taking place globally at the same time also imply that such adoption can have bigger results.

---

[5] https://reader.elsevier.com/reader/sd/pii/S0305750X15002703?token=9A69C55420B2624F49A74640072A9954C953CA6466962F41A8E282CAD60B656EF4A5F63727864E1A45242A51F075A346&originRegion=eu-west-1&originCreation=20210617080816

STEMMING THE GRAIN DRAIN AND HOW TO CREATE A REVERSE FLOW

So we have to tackle this problem in two ways. One is to stem the grain drain caused by the above factors and second is to cause a 'reverse' grain drain, that is, to attract existing social entrepreneurs and also lure commonplace professionals to think of agriculture as a cool path to a prosperous career. Let's look at both of these.

Stem the Grain Drain

I have highlighted eight reasons which contribute to the younger generation leaving the farms, not to mention the lure of the big city and more urbanization itself. While not all the reasons can be altered, there are a few that can be, primarily making it lucrative and increasing the knowledge of the younger generation. Technology can make farming less of a 'physical' task as well as make income more predictable. Land aggregation can address the small size too. I believe that the rest will fall into place automatically once the young farmer is savvy and sees a bright future for themselves, and this 'career' will soon start trending on social media! (It is already starting to.) We are already seeing many articles very glamorously highlighting success stories of rural youth as well as urban professionals quitting their jobs to start farming. The pandemic has also made many a family which were disengaged with farming re-engage. Many were forced to return to villages as they temporarily lost their city jobs. I met one family recently where the father was a driver and the son was a cook and had both returned and re-embraced farming in a positive way, experimenting with growing new crops with better economics. While a negative motivation led to several farmers relooking at farming and adopting modern methods, a positive motivation by the government and other stakeholders can also cause sustainable change in behaviour. Here's what I propose.

1. **Making farming lucrative:** This is the single most powerful way to stop the grain drain. But, of course, it is easier said than done. And this book takes this bull by its horns and dives deep into how it can be done. And agritech and modern methods are key approaches. I have introduced this approach in Chapter 1 and expanded it in Chapters 4 and 5.

2. **Increasing knowledge:** State-owned primary and middle schools in villages which most of the farmers' children attend should offer some basic courses on agriculture, farming and cultivation as compulsory subjects. In fact, some non-profits like Future Agriculture Leaders of India are doing exactly that in states of Maharashtra and Gujarat. Second, the KVKs and extension offices or even the industrial training institutes (ITIs) should offer more advanced courses for vocational training in various aspects of agriculture as well. We already have a start made by the AgriClinics and AgriBusiness Centres (ACABC) scheme with short 45-day vocational courses. Third, to make it more fashionable and acceptable, the AUs and even private sector companies should launch apps targeted at the rural youth to teach various levels of agriculture-related courses in fun ways—some free of cost and some even on a paid basis. If this three-tier structure can by launched and offered, we can have the younger generation which is leaving farming thinking twice before doing so.

Interactions with several stakeholders including prominent agritech venture capitalists have echoed this approach very strongly. Some have gone as far as saying that the compulsory agricultural education in primary and secondary schools should be nationwide and not only restricted to rural areas. Moreover, it should be split into technical agricultural sciences and commercial agribusiness curriculum. They also feel that the social image of an agriculturist needs to be lifted, which some start-ups are doing by hiring the rural youth as their 'on-the-ground entrepreneurs'. I could not agree more.

Reverse Grain Drain

We all know how a hockey-stick-like change can happen once something goes mainstream, that is, a slow start which is followed by a huge positive change once critical mass is achieved. And for farming to go mainstream, it must appeal to a very large number of city dwellers and that too the young and middle-aged adults who are still settling into their careers. It is heartening that in today's times, people are very open-minded and in fact pursuing offbeat career paths. Not only that, but a vibrant private equity (PE) and VC ecosystem enables a lot of start-ups to come up and give their business plans a shot. This in turn generates a lot of employment opportunities for those who are looking at new and exciting careers. There are many middle-aged professionals who are also looking at alternate careers and to switch their career paths. There is a big increase in socially aware entrepreneurs and youth who are very keen to engage in the social sector. The government is also running incubators in many parts of the country, often along with technology institutes.

These are the ingredients of a sustained reverse grain drain—availability of funding for start-ups in this field, increasing number of new businesses entering and enthusiastic young and middle-aged talent to join these companies. The government is also playing a part in talking about reforms and liberalization in agriculture and bringing the conversation mainstream. They are also providing loans and subsidized rates with guarantees and allowing anyone and everyone to be eligible so that the funnel of talent which enters this sector can be widened.

But more can be done. The existing network of AUs in small towns of India is already an existing channel. Maybe if they could set up small extension arms in a few larger cities too, it could be convenient for youth. But an even better way would be to offer agriculture (upstream and downstream) courses in normal colleges. In that context, it is indeed interesting to note that already dozens of business schools in India offer courses 'related' to agriculture such as rural marketing and agribusiness management. While these focus on students who want to join companies selling goods and services to rural India, an expansion of the scope of these courses to more core farming and upstream activity would be a great leg up towards this goal.

The pandemic has forced all of us to introspect and review our career and life choices. Many of us have at least spent some time working from home from a rural or mountain place. And many of us have dreamt of not returning to the cities. The germ of doing something related to farming has been planted in many of us urbanites already! It is indeed a good opportunity to build on.

This chapter laid down the context of the need of accelerating change from various viewpoints, be it retaining the youth or attracting new farmers and suggesting various solutions to do so. We must now answer the question of how this has to be done.

CHAPTER 4

HOW WILL THEY RUN IT?

Ground-up Story: Lack of Government Jobs Bringing Back the Youth!

When I first called Sujay in the afternoon, he was busy at his farm and told me that he would call back in the evening. I felt guilty for disturbing him. Sujay Singh is a farmer from Bhiwani in Haryana and has a 14-acre farm of his own. He is the only one in the family operating the farm. He has spent many years trying to get farmers together into interest groups and clubs to make them work together. He sees a few peculiarities of farmers in Haryana. 'The biggest issue', he says is that farm sizes are 'shrinking very rapidly and are barely 2–2.5 acres today'. I asked him what makes this an issue unique to Haryana because the average farm size in India is also the same. To this he replied that urbanization via infrastructure projects (road and rail) as well as industrial zones had led to a lot of farmers having to sell their land. It is very difficult to get farm labour, too and most come from neighbouring states. The problem is so big that 20 per cent of Haryana farmers are farming in Rajasthan today! I asked him why don't the farmers group up to avoid the problems and challenges of small holdings? He started laughing. 'Sir, farmers in Haryana don't want to get together. They are not happy sharing resources with each other.' If they were to just join some of the new platforms together, things would be better, he said. I was also surprised to hear that despite almost 80 per cent irrigation penetration, only 20 per cent farmers take a third crop. And the reason for not trying to maximize the number of crops grown, in many cases, was the lack of motivation as they were getting by with their current earning and knew that they could fall back on government schemes and kisan loans!

With that, I moved the discussion towards the methods being used and the youth in the villages. 'Parents strongly discourage their children from joining farming, and there is a lot of pressure for them to join city jobs, mostly government jobs. At least till they turn 25, they keep trying. If they fail, then they think of coming back to farming. With recent drop in government job availability, many have been forced to relook at agriculture and that is a good thing.' He felt that children should be made to learn something about farming right from primary school. A few courses should be compulsory. Because by the time they are in high school, they have a mind of their own, and it is very difficult to then attract them back. He told me about a study done recently where they found that all the young children and half the farmers were using smartphones, which means that this group of farmers and their youth must be targeted to learn via technology and then practise modern farming.

'Why don't the KVK officials and extension officers make it a point to involve at least one child from the family when they engage farmers on various technical topics?' I asked. He said that it was a great idea and if such targets were given to these agencies, it could have a big impact. He also felt that more advertising about agriculture targeted towards the youth is needed and vocational training schemes like ACABC should not be limited to few farmers and should be advertised widely.

It was a Friday evening and Sujay had a friend waiting, so I asked my last question and wrapped up the interview: What does he think about mechanization? 'Small holder farmers cannot afford it and don't want to rent it. The only way to convert them is to show success stories of similar size farmers and broadcast it. Seeing is believing. The change in behaviour will spread like fire....'

I drew a lot of insights from this discussion: his ideas about early engagement with the youth, broad-basing vocational training schemes, hard work required to get farmers together and the role 'broadcasting success stories' can play.

With this, I move to the connected topic of 'how' farming needs to be done going forward.

OPENING UP TO POSSIBILITIES AND FARMING SOLUTIONS

Those farmers who decide to stick to farming despite small farms and shortage of farm hands will have to inevitably turn towards more automation and modern methods.

On the one hand, farmers in many parts of the country are optimistic while learning that there is more that can be done in agriculture vs the age-old ways and that there is a real option for them to improve their earnings materially. On the other hand, there is also a strong feeling of despair among others. But my interactions have shown that more of them are open to listening and trying out new methods and practices. Many of my discussions with farmers have shown that farmer families are more positive about their future and looking at their 'profession' with renewed vigour and optimism. In one of my interviews, a farmer told me how he was setting up a small eco-tourism property on his farm to add to his income. That reminded me of what happened in Italy way back in the 1950s and 1960s. The reason Italian agriculture thrived and became a global brand was because farmers there learnt the skill of specialization and of creating a story around their produce which would differentiate even a commodity and allow them to charge premium prices for it. In fact, there were two more striking similarities: (a) the most successful part of

Italian agriculture has happened in the hills and (b) one of the secrets of their success was to build a brand and promote agri-tourism/farm stays.

So if we assume that many farmer families are willing to learn and embrace new methods, then the next question is how one brings about that change. The farmer will need a bit of literacy and basic education and the support of a few of his children who are also interested in getting involved with farming. Once we have two–three people in the family ready and open-minded, the journey can begin. It will need a change of mindset as well.

NEW RULES OF THE GAME

Rather than feeling the need to have to do it, the younger generations will have to be excited and positive about taking it up as their 'career'. I have put a brief framework around this to make it easier to grasp and remember. I call it **the 4 Ps**.

Pride: Rediscover the Pride in the Activity

Currently, if any youth is involved in the family farm, it is usually due to lack of jobs or money and rarely their first choice. Hence, it is important that they understand that they must do it for the right reasons. That small and marginal farming may not be the same as in the past and may need a lot of new energy and impetus. This is where pride comes in. Because weather cycles are getting harsher and resources are getting scarcer, running a small farm is going to be even tougher than the past. But at the same time, due to new tools and methods available, even small farms can be very profitable. (It has been evidenced that yield- and productivity-wise, small farms are already more efficient than larger ones.[1]) Therefore,

---

[1] https://www.hindustantimes.com/india-news/rs-6-000-is-6-of-a-small-farmer-s-annual-income-according-to-nsso-data/story-rddMw0hk6cSbxjo7E1GyKK.html

the journey is going to be more intense. This will need them to have an inherent belief in farming and that they can thrive and flourish in this activity. They must see this as a career choice and not some misfortune which has fallen upon them. It is indeed true and encouraging that with so many urban youths looking to take up modern farming, this activity is becoming quite cool and even socially acceptable.

Sharp Focus on Profitability

The young farmers will have to have a razor-sharp focus on profitability and run it like a tight shop. They cannot run it in a reactive mode. They will have to be proactive about it and seek out higher profits. There are several ways this can be achieved—whether on the revenue side or cost side, as explained before. They will have to equip themselves with the knowledge either by attending a local AU or through courses run by KVKs.

Pursue with Independence: Looking Outside the Government Ecosystem

The third element of this approach is to be independent—independent of the government support. And here I mean mainly with respect to pricing and consequently crop choice but also adopting activities just so that one can get all the subsidy benefits. This mindset needs to change. Once young farmers begin looking at cultivation as a business, and evaluating each decision to maximize profits, rather than reduce effort or risk, a truly independent agribusiness model will emerge. And that is the way forward. Along the way, if suitable and useful government schemes are launched (of which there are many such as grants for solar panels, crop insurance and irrigation), they must use it. Being independent doesn't mean to shun useful resources available. In fact, they will have to be embraced proactively. Extension centres and KVKs have a wealth of knowledge. Sometimes they may not be in proximity (often they are 40–70 km away), but effort should be put to maximize the knowledge gain from all these. Box 4.1 highlights the important role KVKs play as well as how they can help new young farmers learn and succeed.

> **Box 4.1. The Role of KVKs in India**
>
> It is worth noting and understanding the KVK system in India a little better. The first KVK was established in India in 1974, and today there are about 700 such centres in India for a 150 million farmer population. That is one centre covering about 200,000 farmers. That too on an offline basis. Further, the main mandate of a KVK is to act as the dissemination bridge between central research agencies and the end farmer, spreading the relevant, practical, doable part or information and knowledge about the research on agriculture technology.[2] Over the years, KVKs have focused on integrating information and communications technology into their platform to help them spread information on an online basis. But it has had its challenges such as less staff to maintain the data and software and less open-mindedness on the part of farmers to pay too much heed to it all. This is not something limited to India only. It has been seen in most lower-middle income countries, for example, South America and Africa. In both these places, there are examples showing that purely government- or NGO-led farm advisory or consulting technology services seldom last long or achieve scale. A quote from a report by the GSMA on Latin America make this point well, 'Most tools in Latin America continue to be managed by cooperatives or NGOs with limited user numbers, and there have been fewer impact investors helping to scale commercial digital agriculture solutions in

---

[2] https://en.wikipedia.org/wiki/Krishi_Vigyan_Kendra

Latin America.'³ It is my strong belief therefore that private sector coming into this with a profit motive can only run this sustainably. I'll be discussing more of that in later chapters. My proposal is quite different. It is not about spreading the word on research being undertaken but designing more user-friendly workshops on day-to-day modern methods, best practices, mechanization and agritech (sensors, drones and robots), new crop varieties, environment-friendly and resource-friendly precision farming knowledge and design short and long courses (one week to six months) for various levels of farmers' children so that they can get well trained on initial and ongoing bases. I believe that the Indian Council of Agricultural Research (ICAR) along with the various AUs with funding from the government (maybe jointly by education and agriculture ministries) would be the best places to design and launch such courses in various vernacular languages and put it on their online learning platforms. These could also be paid courses and offered even by popular private companies such as Coursera, edX and Udacity.

Paradigm Shift: Be Open to New Ideas

And, finally, young farmers will have to brace for a total paradigm shift. Question and review almost every aspect of their farming activity, right from what they grow and how many crops they grow to how they buy, store, sell and how they organize themselves. There should be no shame in getting together with other like-minded farmers in nearby clusters to innovate and collectively enhance the efficiency of what they do. I have highlighted the Himachal model here in Box 4.2.

---

³ Andrew Shepherd, *Lessons for Sustainability: Failing to Scale ICT4Ag-enabled Services* (Wageningen: Technical Centre for Agricultural and Rural Cooperation ACP-EU (CTA), 2016).

Box 4.2. The Himachal Model

Around 2012–2013, Himachal Pradesh experienced a boom of engineering courses run by private colleges and institutes. It became easy to get admissions for an engineering degree—a very sought-after thing in rural India. No surprises then that a host of young students enrolled, expecting a great career ahead. This led to an oversupply of engineers. And when they graduated in 2017 onwards, the situation was such that there were no jobs. Rather than to keep looking and wasting even more time, some of them realized the opportunity which could be unearthed right in their own farms and orchards. There was a buzz about how apple prices were going up and new varieties could lead to better earnings. A cohort of some 80 engineers from that area got together and improved their understanding and jumped into horticulture. They armed themselves with research, knowledge and even global connectivity to transform their multigenerational family orchards. Today, they have seen their productivity increase manifold because of newer varieties of apples they imported from Spain, which require less spacing (3–4 feet vs 10–12 feet earlier) and start producing in 1–2 years vs 4–5 years in the older varieties. This led to a manifold increase in the revenue per acre for them, and they haven't looked back since! They run their own WhatsApp groups to constantly share best practices and strive for continuous improvement.

The other aspect is about the government which has been very progressive and supportive towards farmers. It provided fairly active machinery at the block and extension levels and was giving high grants and subsidies as much as 40–80 per cent on important tools and equipment needed by farmers, whether it is fencing material to protect their farms from animals or netting to protect trees from the frost.

The third aspect is of several large or experimental farmers readily sharing their success stories and best practices by hosting live workshops for free or even putting up videos on

> their own YouTube channels, which is followed by almost all serious farmers.
>
> This combination of aware youth, communal spirit and a supportive government is what I call the Himachal model—something that other states should replicate.

They must also be open to finding out the various technologies available to them, whether it is farm advisory, farm management, precision farming, etc., and adopt them on their farms. They should realize that even at a small farm level, many of these technologies, best practices and modern methods can be used. I have also heard of stories how in every community there will be one or two farmers who are leading the way, pioneering and using new methods. Most of them are open to sharing their ways. Farmers should be open to this approach and learn from wherever they can. The Farmers Business Network (FBN) is a start-up in the USA, which is just doing that. Wefarm is a similar start-up in the UK, where knowledge sharing by the farmers and for the farmers is the key objective. And both of these are among the successful new agritech start-ups.

Play It Differently

If none of the above is possible, they will have to then be open to renting their land out to those who are willing and able to pursue farming. This brings me back to the topic I mentioned in Chapters 2 and 3—that of land aggregation and land lease laws. In states where farmland tenancy is feasible, young farmers should be open to renting it out, rather than keeping their land fallow and uncultivated. It would be a shame if they choose to neither cultivate themselves nor allow others to do it.

Before I wrap up this chapter, I would like to highlight an important trend which is being seen in many parts of the world. Globally, the overall farmer community is witnessing the increase of young and new farmers. Either it's the second generation taking up their family farm with pride and running it with modern methods or the new young adults taking up farming as a career choice. In fact, both men and women are doing it. In Italy, as per statistics shared in the agribusiness course by the Università Bocconi,[4] about 10 per cent of current farm population is made up of people of below 30 years of age. And about 40 per cent of these are female farmers. This has started happening in India as well but at a very tiny scale (examples of engineers and chartered accountants in Maharashtra and Bihar leaving city jobs and starting farming). I am optimistic that this trend will increase in India as well. We have institutions, technology and government support. Farmer families and other urban youth just need to realize the opportunity which lies in front of them, as agriculture reform and liberalization take hold and create the next few decades of opportunity for the society.

---

[4] Course on 'Challenges of Agribusiness Management' by Università Bocconi, offered on Coursera.

PART III

UNDERSTANDING AGRITECH: THE OLD AND THE NEW

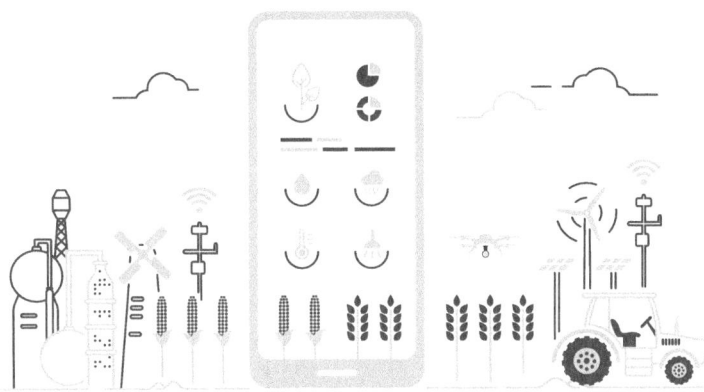

CHAPTER 5

TOWARDS A BROAD DEFINITION OF TECHNOLOGY IN AGRICULTURE

Ground-up Story: Kashmiri Apples, Zaffran and Technology

I had mustered up the courage to visit Kashmir and was going there after nearly 40 years. I wanted to cover the entire country in my research for this book and where better than to start right at the top! It was about 10 degrees around 3 in the afternoon when I started my meetings with local farmers on the outskirts of Srinagar. They were mainly growing apples and saffron but also some vegetables, while some had tree plantations used for wooden furniture, toys and even pencils.

Hamid Ansari was one of the large local farmers and clearly the extrovert in the group. I started engaging him in some discussions about the current technology situation and some questions on the future. The group was on balance, quite proud of what they were doing and felt that they had more potential to produce and market. They felt that they had a 'brand' which they could differentiate and sell widely and get better pricing for their produce.

Even about the future, they had already experimented with some indigenous machines, and he simplified it for me by saying that in the past they used machines for grading and sorting their produce and that these machines were indigenously made. But they were few and far between and meant that the farmers had to lug their produce quite a distance to get them sorted. But he also said that the main effort goes into plucking. And that must be done manually. He was keen to understand if there was a cheap and reliable solution for that. He was very happy to hear that there were such machines getting developed, and I gave him the example of Tevel, an Israeli company which has launched such machines for apple harvesting. I shared the picture promptly to his WhatsApp and he said that he would like to explore how it works.

What surprised me was their general optimism and pride and that even apple farmers in Kashmir had gotten the whiff of technology and were willing to engage in a deeper discussion on what could be done and how. They were not only open to hearing me out but also excited and enthused by what I had to say and were very willing to give technology and modern practices a fair chance. I felt that the demand for new automation devices is probably much more than people think!

A HOLISTIC APPROACH TO AGRITECH

I sometimes worry that we may overwhelm the farmers by overusing the word agritech as the cure for all ailments, which it may very well be, but to look at technology in a very limited and geeky way would be a mistake. I also strongly believe that agritech should be seen and defined in a very broad way, more as a modern agricultural system which stands for all and any new approaches of engaging in the entire spectrum of agricultural activities, which helps to enhance the overall earnings of the farmer within his existing constraints (land size, weather, water availability, market access, etc.).

The reason for this approach is also that each of these so-called, routine, traditional activities can have as transformational an impact as any new technology. If we go by this definition, then we can start diving deeper into all aspects of modern agriculture and not just some hot buzzwords. In fact, this chapter serves that very purpose of defining agritech. So throughout the book, we can use this understanding as we outline various solutions which are available or needed for the Indian farmer.

The Process of Change Must Start with the Seed

As one would imagine, any change has to start with the seed. It is true even more so for agriculture. Using better varieties of seed is one thing, but also knowing the cultivation process of such newer seeds is important to get the full benefit out of its higher yield or robustness. One of the KVK heads I was speaking to said that the seed has the highest return on investment (ROI) for a farmer. Because easily a 20 or even 30 per cent yield improvement occurs from better seeds with almost no follow-up, training or other scientific processes required. Mechanization and precision farming may need a lot of investments and training, but using a better seed properly is the easiest thing to teach and get a fast, tangible result out of it. A farmer in Jharkhand told me that access for farmers to hybrid seeds would be a big boost to their ecosystem.

Followed by Crop Selection

This may sound very basic, but it is surprising how most farmers don't even think of this as a problem they are solving for. I mentioned this briefly in a previous chapter too. As in this is not a variable they even review. It is assumed to be a given. They have been growing a particular mix of crops for years or even decades because of an age-old practice. And hence they assume that it is the best crop they can grow, given their soil quality and other agronomic conditions. They do not see value in questioning or reviewing this. As a professional businessman, this clearly cannot be the case. There are a few key elements which determine what a farmer can grow. It's firstly their location and the climatic conditions around their farm. Second, it is the soil that their farm area has. A third element would be the amount of acreage on which a particular crop has been planted in the previous/current season and lastly the prices achieved for it. In fact, the weather is even less important, as irrigation, water harvesting and greenhouses can often allow the farmer to push the envelope a bit on that. Successful growth of mushrooms in the upper reaches and of apples in the lower reaches of Himachal are good examples. In any case, it boils down to just the weather, soil and market information. If just these three were the only inputs in the decision-making process, the options available to any farmer would be immense. But the farmer adds into their mix exogenous factors such as: (a) Whether the crop is part of the government MSP? (b) Can they sell it at the nearest *mandi?* and (c) What are their neighbours growing? Such aspects colour their crop selection decision. I think agritech and modern farming should mean that this decision is only governed by scientific inputs. Any service which enables this, to my mind, is a starting point of agritech.

Multicropping Can Multiply Income

Usually, a farmer grows one crop a year which takes about six–nine months from the sowing to the harvesting cycle. If they are a little more motivated and are covered by irrigation, they would take two crops of six-monthly cycles each. Very rarely do we see farmers doing three crop cycles via intercropping or growing some shorter cycle crops. On average, 40 per cent of the farms grow more than 1 crop. But in most states, this number is much lower at 25 per cent, which means that 75 per cent of farmland is lying unused for 6 months a year! There is hence a lot of scope for improving this. Usually, it is difficult to take multiple crops in rainfed areas but otherwise it is technically and technologically possible to do three or even four crops. Usually, lack of awareness or motivation stops farmers from doing it. Another reason which stops them from doing this is lack of access to technology and affordability. At times, to take multiple crops, one needs to invest in machines and advanced storage solutions, so that crops which are cut slightly earlier than usual have a safe and controlled place, where they can be dried and stored. You also need machines to pull out the residual stump of the previous crop and technology to prepare the soil for the next crop. Sometimes the moisture in the soil may be more or less than needed. Hence, it may have to be treated to get it prepared and brought into the right shape. All this needs technology and modern practices as well as larger investments.

	Global (Till 2002)	India
All arable land (million hectare)	1160	150
Irrigated land (%)	20	49
Total multicropped land	134.4 million hectares[a]	12%
Cropping intensity (x)	1.1	1.4[b]
Upside from multicropping	89–398 million hectare	7%–30%
India penetration	40%–60% take more than 1	16%–25% based on irrigation/39%[c]

Table 5.1. Global Multicropping Penetration

Source: https://www.cgiar.org/news-events/news/multiple-cropping-could-help-feed-the-world/
Notes: [a]130 m is 2 crops and only 4 m hectare is 3 crops.
[b]https://www.drishtiias.com/daily-updates/daily-news-analysis/groundwater-depletion-and-cropping-intensity
[c]39% as per some estimates (report on doubling farmers' income by Ramesh Chand); anecdotal and looks high because maybe there are more small farmers in India who need it more.

Table 5.1 above draws attention to the global scenario on multicropping and how big an upside is seen from further improvements. Note that India has a much higher cropping intensity than the world average (could be due to the higher number of small farmers and higher than world average irrigation (49% vs 20%), and it has been growing over the years from 123.1 per cent in 1980–1981 to 141.5 per cent in 2015–2016.[1]

Mechanization: Tractors, Farm Equipment and Irrigation Are Not Passe

One may feel that why should one focus on old world things such as a tractor, farm equipment and even irrigation. Aren't they passe? Should a chapter on agritech be talking about this? Well, there are a few key points here. First, in many ways mechanization is at the heart of a lot of the agritech progress. Most high-tech gadgets actually get fixed on top of a tractor. Many precision farming techniques involve irrigation systems as their base. Basic mechanization is indeed a building block for more advanced solutions. Hence, increasing their penetration on Indian farms is crucial before hoping for newer things. Second, the penetration of these machines is only 40–45 per cent and hence the impact of using these 'basic' machines can also be large. There are two reasons for the low penetration, affordability being the main one, followed by awareness of all the benefits. We need a solution for both.

Especially the total cost of ownership of tractors and equipment can be brought down by creating renting and sharing models. I called it the uberization of farm equipment in my previous book *A Wall Street View of Rural India*. It is also being called 'farming as a service' or FaaS. There are various companies which have started offering this as aggregators of demand. And very recently, the Central government has announced that through the CHCs in villages, farm equipment will be available for hire where the CHC will directly provide the equipment. This can be very powerful and should not

---

[1] http://www.fao.org/fileadmin/user_upload/FAO-countries/India/docs/Full_Paper-1.pdf

be underestimated. But on the supply side too, some work is yet to be done because unlike a taxi, demand for a tractor is quite bunched up during the same sowing and harvesting days during the year. So scheduling optimization in clusters with some crop cycle diversity would be needed as a smart solution to make even the renting business model viable on a commercial scale.

Doing More with Less: Precision Farming Mantra

If one divides the spectrum of farming activities into 'to the farm', 'at the farm' and 'from the farm', these three slices sum up all the farming activities. It is instructional to note that the maximum scope for change lies *at the farm* and not at input or output stages. But most of the technological developments globally and in India and the start-ups and VC investments have mainly gone into the 'to the' and 'from the' farm segments, leaving the actual farm relatively neglected. That is where precision farming comes into play. It is basically technology which helps to reduce the use of inputs (land, seeds, water, power, labour, fertilizers and pesticides) while also boosting yields and output. All resources at the farm are always in short supply, starting from the land itself; hence, much more attention needs to be given to this.

Again, I define 'at the farm' technology quite broadly, including best practices of crop selection, soil analysis and use of appropriate intercropping. Let me outline a list, which by no means is exhaustive but will give you a flavour of the scope of what this involves.

1. Regular soil analysis to know what all crops can be grown well and catch any destruction in soil structure and optimize nutrient use so it can be addressed.

2. Choice of crops which need less moisture and nutrients or are hardy and need less pesticides or herbicides—sturdy crops.

3. Choice of seed which has high productivity and better variety which can fetch better prices.

4. Water conservation, which can be done by making drains and ditches, canals and roadbed catchments. It can also be done by using Internet-of-things (IoT)-based sensors which measure the moisture level in the soil and allow the farmer to water accordingly (avoid over watering and runoffs). We also have drones and sensors as well as satellite and GIS-based systems which can look at the farm and crops, cloud formations, wind direction and, of course, the weather forecast and help the farmer choose when to not water their crop if it is going to rain soon, and to protect their crop if bad weather is expected.

5. Nutrient conservation—an important way to avoid loss of natural nutrients of the soil is to avoid runoff, which can be done by following the suggestions made in the previous point above. On top of that, sensors can also read nutrient content in soil and let farmer add only in the quantities precisely needed. A third way of doing this is by using no-till farming. This topic is of great relevance and hence I will devote a few paragraphs to it separately later in this chapter. Even multicropping leads to lower use of fertilizers.

6. Pesticide use minimization—we can reduce herbicides use, if we deploy manpower to manually remove the weeds. But that could be expensive. Or some tools can be used attached to the tractor to remove them. So a mix of herbicides, labour and machinery can optimize spend on pesticides. Technology is available via machine vision and artificial intelligence (AI), drones (elaborated later in the chapter) and sensors, which can by the look of a crop roots or leaves predict disease long before it starts affecting them. This can lead to lesser pesticide use due to early detection and lesser crop damage. Smart spraying technology uses smaller droplet sizes to precisely apply

pesticides, and it can reduce usage by up to 50 per cent as well. (If this sounds too futuristic, there are companies which are indeed offering all this!)

7. Another farming practice increasingly getting popular is ZNCF, which basically uses all natural and organic matter already produced on the farm as water, pesticide and fertilizer. This not only makes it environment-friendly and organic but also reduces costs dramatically. This has been promoted in some parts of India already, but adoption has been very low.

8. Rainwater harvesting and solar panels on the farm can also reduce costs of farming.

No-till Farming/Organic Farming and Other Best Practices

It has been old wisdom all over the world that while sowing new crop/seeds, the farm was 'tilled'. Tilling is the process by which the soil is prepared for sowing by overturning the soil and digging. It leads to removal of weeds as well as mixing of nutrients. Cultivators and tillers (machines) were used extensively to do this activity globally, while in the lower-middle income countries bullock/oxen with ploughing tools attached on them would be used. In the 1980s, however, farmers, AUs and scientists learnt that the practice of tilling was doing more harm than good, as it was spoiling the topsoil and soil structure and hence reducing long-term productivity. This gave birth to no-till or low-till farming, which is the main way of doing it in most high-income countries since the last few decades. For example, Australia started following it about 20 years ago, and now 95 per cent of farming is done on a no-till basis. Key benefits are that it prevents soil erosion due to wind, retains the moisture in the soil and gives higher yields due to timely or early seeding made possible due to the retained moisture. On the flip side, 'no-till' increases weed growth, which needs more herbicides use and to which the weeds can also become resistant. Soil compaction is another side effect too. Still, on balance, it is considered best practice for longer-term benefits of soil structure and retention of the topsoil and its fertility—the main asset of a farmer. My research has shown me that no-till farming has been very selectively tried on a pilot basis in a very small part of the country, and it has not succeeded and currently practically no one follows it. The reason cited for this is the soil type in India. If soil is hard, it becomes difficult to use these machines. And the second reason is, of course, low level of mechanization to use such sowing machines in the first place.

Organic farming is another progressive (but traditional in India) way to adopt at a larger scale and can lead to rapid uplift in realizations for farmers from the same plot of land as well as reduce longer-term environmental impact. Organic farming needs a key input though, which is traceability. And that's where agritech can play a crucial role.

At the Factory Gate: Warehousing and Market Access

Once the produce is ready, another set of challenges starts, that is, to get the produce to the market at the lowest cost and sell it at the maximum realization. There are a lot of hoops to go over before the produce reaches the end consumer and, at every stage, some markup gets added. Many start-ups globally and in India are trying to reduce the number of intermediaries so that both the end consumer and the farmer benefit with a little more price to the farmer and a little less cost to the end consumer. Even the government has laid down laws to liberalize the supply chain so that the farmer can improve their market access. The farmer should be open to such new 'players' and models to increase their realization. Even laws on contract farming allow farmers direct access to the buyers and can lead to certainty, visibility and better prices, which can enable the farmer to take a longer-term view and invest in their farm as well. Another way technology and best practices can be adopted is the dedicated procurement channels which some corporates have adopted. ITC's e-Choupal is one such example, where the company directly procures from the farmer and helps them with better prices via appropriate grading and weighing with lower transportation costs. This is not 'contract-farming' but 'assurance farming', a term I recently learnt from an agritech start-up founder. Contract farming is another part of modernizing agriculture. We also have the eNAM electronic marketplace of the government which enables a farmer to sell nationally at the best price possible.

Another important part of the 'from the farm' value chain is warehousing or storage solutions. Currently, India has two sets of storage solutions: first, the warehouses run by the FCI, which mainly cater to storing the grains procured for PDS as well as to store the crop procured by the government under their MSP programme, and the second is the private warehouses built either to ease the shortage faced by FCI (under contract) or to cater to other private buyers (traders and exporters). All this infrastructure is clearly focused on the buyers, government or private sector, and not really on the seller (read: farmer). There is some storage infrastructure of the government meant for the small farmers which is sprinkled around small farming areas, but either they are not in a usable condition or farmers are not much aware of them. Even within the private sector storage, some is offered to farmers and has been taken up too, but after years it remains about a tenth of such space.

Why is this storage so important? For non-perishable crops, if market prices are low due to short-term transitional reasons (e.g., large flush of produce from neighbouring villages or unexpectedly high planting of a crop in a season), a farmer rarely has the chance to 'postpone' their sale and wait for a better price. This is where cheap, accessible storage solutions can be of great help, as it will give them some bargaining power to not offload their produce at the clearing price. Even for perishable horticultural products, some cold storage solutions for the small farmer are needed. Another benefit of such storage is that it allows the farmer to borrow against their stock if they have to store it for a longer period. The Warehousing Development and Regulatory Authority (WDRA) is totally focused on this and works closely with the Central and State Warehousing Corporations as well as with National Commodity and Derivatives Exchange (NCDEX)-promoted National Collateral Management Services Ltd (NCML) to encourage farmers to use these warehouses and how they can use electronic warehouse receipts to monetize their stocks. Some players are registering their warehouse space into this forum. But both space and financing are in short supply and need to increase but even the take-up of what is available is not very high. Farmers should explore these options actively and seek them out as well. We know how demand can create its own supply. Hence, there is a big opportunity for start-ups and farmers to address this infrastructure gap.

Sadly, all these new solutions have not found many takers. Most of these platforms do not have more than 10–15 million farmers. On a base of more than 150 million, that is miniscule.

Contract farming and eNAM are two very important and large subjects, and I will dwell into both in details in the following chapters when I outline the landscape of Indian agritech.

What You (In)put Is What You Get: Input Procurement

If we focus on the 'to the farm' part of best practices, we are talking about the inputs which come into the farm from outside to help the farmer grow their crops. They are seeds, fertilizers and pesticides on the variable cost side and, of course, equipment such as tractors, tools and irrigation systems on the capital cost side. Here, we will focus on the small and marginal farmers as they are the bulk of the farmers in the country. Currently, each farmer procures these inputs at (a) an individual level and (b) from the local dealer or distributor in their village or feeder town (town nearest to his village). Clearly, their bargaining power is almost nil, as the seller has a near monopoly being the only supplier and the buyer is buying extremely small quantities.

A few things can change here with minimal disruption. (a) Buyer aggregation: Buyers can get together to buy in bulk and gain some negotiation power. Buyer aggregation can happen in a more structured way through the FPOs or farmer collectives too. (b) The individual farmer can go to an online marketplace to buy from dozens if not hundreds of sellers to get the cheapest price (easily few per cent lower). There are already many marketplaces online where the farmer can register themselves and buy. This is true for both variable and capex items. What is not fully evolved yet is the buyer aggregation. And I believe that that is where a lot of value can be added. This is a business opportunity for entrepreneurs as well as farmers themselves to organize themselves.

Drones and Robots Are Coming to a Farm Next to You

Let's now talk about the more 'cool' part of agritech, the part which has the maximum buzz—drones and robots.

Drones

This is something which is already being deployed in India to some extent. The first time I heard about it was in 2015 where a company in the weather forecasting business was launching drones to help insurance companies who were selling crop insurance (to help them in claims) and banks (to help them to assess credit risk, loan limits, etc.). Since then, many more companies have started offering similar data services on weather, wind and pest attacks via the use of drones. Drones are basically used for taking pictures of the farm and crops, as well as for spraying chemicals. But again, as always, most of this was launched from a B2B perspective rather than a B2C (C meaning farmer here) perspective, as the farmer is small and may not be able to invest in such solutions and, given a small farm, may not even need it just for themselves. Increasingly though, these services are being offered to farmers directly as part of a subscription service (we talked about FaaS earlier on) bundled with other data analysis (e.g., market price). Farm Friend is a Beijing-based FaaS company, aggregating and renting out drones to farmers, for example.

Robots or Automation

This is an emerging space even globally but is progressing quite rapidly. We can classify this also into two parts.

- **Post-harvest:** This refers to machines used to sort the produce based on quality grades, size, etc., and to pack them into cartons which are ready to be transported.

- **Pre-harvest:** This refers to machines being used for levelling the field, sowing, no-till cultivation, irrigating, spraying pesticides, removing weeds and, of course, in harvesting.

New machines to reduce manual intervention are slowly being developed, tried out and deployed. These machines include harvesters for horticulture; for example, harvesting is difficult and mostly needs manual plucking and is very labour intensive. The reason it needs manual plucking is because very high precision is required to pluck a fruit or vegetable. For a machine to be able to do that, it has to be very advanced. Machine vision and AI are needed to know and keep learning what is ripe, to be picked and to not pluck the wrong thing. This makes the machines quite expensive. Plus, they will need to be customized to local conditions. But there are several companies which are also developing some machines indigenously even as imported machines also get cheaper. So adoption can start in India through a FaaS service or even via an FPO buying it as a shared investment. I have attempted to list down some of the most usable imported and locally made machines across functionalities which can be the first level of automation adoption at the Indian farm (in Chapters 6 and 8).

Information Is King: Weather, Price, Acreage, Pests and Traceability

Just information itself can bring a revolution for the farmer. It has been talked about for years and gained more mindshare once 4G and the smartphones became cheap and ubiquitous in rural India. This has got a further fillip by the BharatNet[2] and DigiGaon[3] initiatives of the government to provide high-speed fibre optic connectivity to all villages and farmers. Primarily, there are three areas where information can help the farmer in a big way. 'Weather', of course, is the major factor. Short-term forecasts (up to 14 days) about rain can help the farmer plan their sowing activities as well as regulate their water usage at the farm. Early warning of unseasonal rains or delayed monsoons can help immensely as well. Second, the farmer cares about 'acreage', that is, who is planting what. This is more difficult to get intel on (as it depends more on data collection from all farmers), but there are services offering this too. The farmer based on acreage of a particular crop (say sugarcane) can decide to grow a different crop or less of a crop so that during harvest they do not face oversupply at the *mandi* and lower realizations. 'Price information' at various *mandis* and on various platforms is very important for the farmer. They can be smart about where to sell their produce

---

[2] https://telecom.economictimes.indiatimes.com/news/centre-allocates-rs-19041-crore-for-bharatnet-expansion/83920889
[3] https://www.digital-village.in

because as we saw above, they usually do not have storage access. When initially the telecom and digital revolution started a few years ago, there was hope and expectation of an explosion of information services which would be launched and adopted by the farmer. Unfortunately, neither happened. Only a few services were launched and even lesser were adopted. All the bandwidth and high speeds were used up watching cricket or movies on YouTube. 'Disease prevention information' is another service which is useful. In this, the service provider installs devices which through spectral and orthopotic photography can forewarn the farmer about potential pest attacks or even diseases which may spread on their farm. Another agritech service which can be classified under information is 'traceability tracking' solutions using technologies such as AI and blockchain.

Fintech

Fintech is another important part of the agritech landscape. And many of the newer techniques will also need some ability of the farmer to spend. This makes fintech also like a building block for other agritech adoption. Small farmers usually struggle to get loans for working capital or capital expenditure outside the KCC scheme. If they do, it is at high rates from the banking system (rarely) or the informal money lenders (more often). Technology can be used to get detailed micro-level data on the individual farmers land, crop output history, weather-related data and past data on pest attacks, and all this when put through advanced algorithms and data crunching can help such fintech companies predict income and underwrite lending risk more efficiently and package sachet-size loans to farmers at cheaper rates. Digital credit scores based on a farmer's social behaviour and other spending patterns helps lenders create robust profiles. Similarly, insurance companies can also extend coverage of wider things at a lower cost based on such smart data gathering and analysis. I am yet to meet a farmer who has told me about a successful crop insurance claim from the traditional system! So there is a big gap here. Such coverage and protection will increase risk appetite of the farmers and allow them to venture out and take cropping decisions more on commercial terms and less on government procurement and MSP and hence follow a more lucrative cultivation programme. Such risk appetite is currently lacking in farmers or has been reducing over the years.

Farming Advisory: Bringing It All Together

That brings me to the last one—farming advisory, a new and novel service being offered to farmers by some private entrepreneurs. It basically involves a very holistic offering, covering all aspects of running the farm in a professional way. It can be looked at as farm management being outsourced to an external professional company. It includes consultancy on crops and farming techniques as well as market access solutions and guidance on available and suitable technologies, among other things. Although the government has been offering some of the advisory services through its own extension offices and KVKs, the reach and frequency have been limited. The government has to increase the number of such advisors and the number of centres they are available at as well as how frequently they visit farms or hold open houses to which farmers can visit. Although private entrepreneurs have also jumped into this, more should focus on this, as it is an asset light annuity kind of business model. What has not yet been explored is how the pricing can be dynamic and hybrid. Pricing can consist of a mix of fixed and variable fees based on benefits to the farmers. We often read that some start-ups have deployed their solutions at hundreds of farms, and farmers are seeing big benefits (e.g., 50% higher output with 50% lesser input costs), yet these companies are probably still making losses. Failed innovative companies will do no one any good. Innovation must be sustainable to have a lasting impact.

Hence, pricing and a path to profitability are crucial. They should explore hybrid revenue models to ensure their own viability. From a farmer's perspective, the entry cost must be kept low but not zero. And because a farmer only believes in what they see and because a crop cycle is too long to wait for in terms of a sales cycle, low entry cost is key. Innovative pricing models which can address this and take a share of the upside will be more palatable to the farmer to make them adopt and embrace these solutions much faster and help service providers be commercially viable. Currently, the FaaS and farm advisory services are at an infant stage of evolution themselves or are being offered by larger agribusiness companies as one of many things they do. And it may even be a free service to get the farmer into their ecosystem. I personally feel that dedicated FaaS companies which focus on scaling their business while making money would be a win-win situation, as they would increase penetration and add to overall productivity at the farm.

CONCLUSION

It is, hence, clear that agritech can be defined in a very broad way, and there is a lot for the farmer to learn and adopt and for the government or the entrepreneur to commercialize and offer. It is indeed a fascinating topic, and we will dwell more into it in the following chapters. I hope that this chapter has made agritech a simpler-to-understand topic. In my next chapter, I further slice and dice agritech and put it into different buckets, so that the reader really visualizes the whole spectrum of technologies in a much more thorough manner, and no important aspect of the value chain is missed out, as I also step deeper into this topic.

CHAPTER 6

SLICING AND DICING TECHNOLOGY

Ground-up Story: *Chakbandi* and Monkey Business

The farmers who had gathered to meet me in a small village in Uttarakhand were excited but also a bit wary as to what I was going to ask them. But once we got talking, they were at ease and were happy to answer my questions, and we got into quite a detailed discussion. Nali was a 30-year-old third-generation farmer, and Narayan Singh was in his 40s and a second-generation farmer. They both owned 2–3 acres each, on which they mainly grew vegetables, some herbs and lemons, as well as wheat, rice and pulses. The soil and weather permitted more horticultural products such as oranges, apples and walnuts, but they were quite bogged down with several problems and hence not pursuing it. Nali mentioned that when his grandfather was operating the same farm, he cultivated on the entire plot and took two–three crops a year. With shortage of labour and water, Nali now barely takes one crop, and his income from the same land has dropped by 60–70 per cent! The second issue they both highlighted was of the menace of monkeys coming and destroying/eating their crop. And the government was not helping by providing subsidized nets or finance for fencing or even stopping the monkey menace. Even if they did the fencing, it would not help due to the third issue—since their land parcels were not contiguous but scattered across, it was not viable to spend on fencing. Hence, they kept watchmen to watch their farms. Not all neighbouring farmers wanted to spend even on that! It's called *chakbandi,* meaning redistributing land to farmers on contiguous basis, as Narayan Singh told me. The monkey business and scattered holdings were news to me. While I stood up to wrap up our meeting, Narayan Singh mentioned to me that he was very keen that his kids get education on latest agriculture techniques and how they could improve their incomes with what they had. He said that he was in regular touch with his block development officer (BDO) and extension officer but was keen to go a step further to learn more. His teenage children were also enthusiastic to learn, although at times they wondered that with all the hard work, whether the returns would be commensurate. Nali also added that the local *sarpanch* had not engaged very closely with the community farmers and usually was more focused on his own farm or work. When I spoke to them about FPOs or KVKs and new business models which would allow even small farmers to do much better, they said that they would like to pursue modern methods but needed advice and handholding. They felt that CF was not so easy to achieve because 'everyone thinks differently!'

I left it at that and wrapped up the meeting. As I walked out of the room, I strongly felt that there were so many nuances to progressive farming but a long way to go to share the knowledge and make them adopt.

In the previous chapter, we have already described the very broad sweep and scope of technology in agribusiness. I have dedicated another chapter with an objective of looking at it in a few different ways, to enhance our understanding. Other institutions have calibrated and segmented agritech in some other ways too. I highlight a few of them here for readers.

1. The WEF[1] in its report has called it the 'transformative twelve'—twelve technologies which are shaping a major change in agriculture and have the potential to have a lasting impact. These 12 technologies give us a sense of how we can classify the value chain: (a) alternative proteins, (b) food sensing, (c) nutrigenetics, (d) big data and advanced analytics, (e) mobile service delivery, (f) blockchain-enabled traceability, (g) IoT, (h) precision agriculture, (i) microbiome technologies, (j) gene-editing for multi-trait seeds, (k) bio-based nutrients and (l) renewable energy.

2. Inc42[2] in its report has classified it as (a) farm inputs, (b) farming cultivation and harvesting (included precision agriculture, FaaS, automation and farm infrastructure), (c) distribution and transportation, (d) postproduction processing and handling, (e) market linkage and (f) financial services.

3. AgFunder[3] has put it in the following buckets: (a) biotech, (b) marketplaces, (c) farm management software, sensing and IoT, (d) robotics, mechanization and equipment, (e) midstream technologies (safety traceability, transportation and logistics), (f) novel farming systems—indoor, urban farming, (g) fintech, (h) innovative food and (i) in-store retail and restaurant tech.

4. The Thrive SVG Forbes[4] study maps the landscape across five segments: (a) controlled environment agriculture, (b) robotics and automation, (c) data and farm management, (d) biotechnology and (e) diary and cattle related.

---

[1] World Economic Forum, *Innovation with a Purpose*.
[2] https://inc42.com/reports/indias-agritech-market-landscape-report-2021/
[3] https://agfunder.com/research/2021-AgFunder-agrifoodtech-investment-report/
[4] https://thriveagrifood.com/wp-content/uploads/2020/03/3.24.20_FINAL-TOP-50-AGTECH-REPORT-.pdf

VALUE CHAIN AND BEST AGRITECH PRACTICES

This chapter not only goes a step deeper into technology but also further simplifies this by explaining it in easy-to-understand ways. I have also attempted to give examples of existing leading companies and explain their offerings to give a very relatable understanding of the technology in Tables 6.1 to 6.7. To enable the reader to draw a mind map of it all, I am segmenting it to give a different perspective.

I hence revisit the various parts of the value chain and populate each with technology changes which are occurring in that segment. I also want to show here that partly by design and partly by default, current progress globally and in India has tended to cluster around a few 'hot pockets' as I call them. Certain technologies cannot be directly used by the farmer; hence, I have kept it out of the scope of this book.

1. **Inside the gate and outside:** I particularly like this definition and way of looking at technology in agribusiness. It basically questions whether an activity is done inside the farm gate or outside. I have further divided this into three parts: 'to the farm', 'at the farm' and 'from the farm'.

    a. **To the farm:** This primarily covers all that a farmer must bring to their farm to start and continue their farming activity. So it would start with seeds, fertilizers, pesticides and machines. This could also include advisory and FaaS services, which are inputs 'coming to' the farm, as well as other analytical inputs such as soil analysis and testing.

    Some of the well-known start-ups in this space are as follows.

Company	Country	Details
Pivot Bio	USA	Efficient nitro-fertilizer preparation and delivery mechanism
Apollo Agriculture	Kenya	Advisory, including for inputs
Terramera	Canada	Plant-based fertilizers and pesticides
Farmers Business Network	USA	Farmer-to-farmer resource-, input- and knowledge-sharing portal
Wefarm	UK	Farmer-to-farmer resource-, input- and knowledge-sharing portal
Abundant Robotics	USA	Harvesting machines for apple orchards (machines which pluck the fruit)
Uller	Brazil	App used for renting farm equipment from larger farmers
Agrofy	Brazil	Marketplace for machinery and equipment mainly
Indigo	USA	Focuses on microbiomes (beneficial bacteria); identifies and uses them to coat seeds, which strengthens and makes plants hardy
Growers Edge	USA	Financial services company providing insurance and access to capital
Esoko	Africa	Operates in nine countries; price info and marketplace; does scout polling on inventories, crop activities, crop cycles and yields

Table 6.1. Well-known Start-ups in 'To the Farm'

Source: https://hexgn.com/top-agritech-startups-2019/

b. **At the farm:** This relates to the core activity of cultivation, that which the farmer conducts on the farm daily, that is, sowing, watering, applying the fertilizer and pesticides, monitoring the crop for damage due to animals, thieves or a disease, harvesting, threshing, drying, sorting, grading and storing. Entire precision agriculture, FaaS, farm management and farm advisory get included in this category.

Company	Country	Details
Plenty	USA	Vertical, indoor, urban farming
Bowery	USA	Vertical, indoor, urban farming
Ceres Imaging	USA	Precision farming—improving efficiencies of irrigation systems with the help of aerial spectral imaging by monitoring their health
Conservis	USA	Farm management software to manage, plan orders, inventory, storage, delivery as well as yield analysis and forecasting
BrightFarms	USA	Vertical, indoor, urban farming
Infarm	Germany	Vertical, indoor, urban farming; decentralized on a global basis; hosting farms at supermarkets
Prospera	Israel	Precision farming—using central pivot irrigation systems for smart farming
FarmLogs	USA	Farm-based data management and analytics
Gotham Greens	USA	Vertical, indoor, urban farming
Taranis	Israel	Data management for pest and diseases
Farm66	Hong Kong	Urban farming, supplying fresh produce to supermarkets

Table 6.2. Well-known Start-ups in 'At the Farm'

c. **From the farm:** This is the piece which takes place outside the farm gate after the farmer's produce is ready to be shipped out. There are several parts to this story, starting from short-term storage. This storage is different from on-the-farm storage, which is done for maybe further processing or dehumidifying before packing, etc. The storage outside the farm is when the produce is ready to be taken to the market to sell. But there may be reasons why the timing may not be right, or transportation may not be available or the weather may be bad. So short-term storage comes first and can be closely coupled with financing. Transportation comes next, followed by access to a market. This could be a physical market or an online one. This could be a contracted-out supply or a normal direct sale. It could be to an agent, wholesaler, trader, exporter, retailer or the end consumer. Another part of transportation is the traceability part which is linked to food safety and provides farmers potential for premium pricing which is done by using blockchain technologies and QR codes. In fact, two-way traceability is possible, and the farmer also gets to see where their produce went and what portion of the end price they received.

Company	Country	Details
Meicai	China	Selling produce online via a marketplace
Produce Pay	USA	Resources to help farmers access marketplace and customers
Apeel	USA	Produce freshness enhancers to reduce PHLs and increase shelf/storage life of the produce
Safe Traces	USA	Traceability

Table 6.3. Well-known Start-ups in 'From the Farm'

2. **Below the ground vs above the ground:** This is another way of visualizing the landscape of agricultural technologies available to farmers, albeit more focused on precision farming.

   Below the ground: This area includes devices using IoT and sensors which monitor the state of the soil and help to advise just-in-time and just-the-right quantity and quality of inputs which the crop needs (water, fertilizer, pesticides, biomes and maybe even salinity, etc.). And this part of agritech is still not very advanced. Moisture-reading sensors are more widely available, but for other aspects, things are still developing. Even the moisture-reading apparatus has levels of ease of use, which are still also getting streamlined. But if one were to understand 'below the ground' in a little wider sense, it then includes even the seeds which go in the entire biotech space, sowing technologies and approaches like 'no till', for example, and even nutrient management solutions and soil management services.

Company	Country	Details
CropX	Israel	Precision agriculture—below-the-ground sensors monitoring soil moisture, nutrients and disease; the company does above the ground too
Farmers Edge	USA	Precision agriculture but using more above-the-ground sensors on tractors and satellite imagery and cloud-based big data to give farmers decision support tools
Agrosmart	Brazil	Generates market intelligence and creates agronomic models based on seed genetics, soil type and microclimate; combines ground truth data and best-in-class analytical capabilities to provide actionable insights for a more productive and sustainable agriculture
Arable Labs	USA	A data company which powers better decisions in agriculture through an integrated approach to hardware, software and data science
Resson	Canada	Integrated decision farming company using AI, cloud, sensors, drones and satellite and near-field cameras to give holistic insights to farmers on yield, pests, weather, etc.

Table 6.4. Well-known Start-ups in 'Below the Ground'

Above the ground: On the other hand, 'above-the-ground' technologies will include a host of areas like the more traditional things such as irrigation, tractors, harvesters, threshing machines and the more advanced above-the-ground sensors, GPS, GIS solutions (for weather data or optical sensors with machine vision which can alert or pest attacks or even other animal attacks). Going even further, this would include robots and drones which are using data on the cloud and carrying on activities on the farm.

Company	Country	Details
MagGrow	Ireland	Pesticide-spraying technology company; focuses on minimizing the size of the droplets so maximum spray can reach and stay on the plant, thereby reducing pesticide use and saving water too

Table 6.5. Well-known Start-ups in 'Above the Ground'

3. **Pre-harvest vs post-harvest:** This is a very popular way of categorizing.

    a. **Pre-harvest technologies:** We would put things like almost the entire 'on-the-farm' technologies as well as the 'below-the-ground' technologies into the pre-harvest space. Even the 'to-the-farm' category would get included here.

    b. **Post-harvest:** We need to get more specific on the post-harvest front though. Post-harvest can be divided into three areas. (a) One is the harvesting process itself, which will mainly include all the harvesting machines (not only normal combined harvesters but also robotic advanced harvesting machines). (b) The second category would be technology for then threshing the produce, drying, handling and on-farm storage, sorting, grading and packing it. This will include systems and approaches to reduce PHLs, which is a big subject I have included in the book elsewhere. Given the fact that PHL can be as high as 30–50 per cent of produce across crops and geographies, it is a very high ROI solution. (c) We then move into the space of 'at-the-gate' or 'from-the-farm' technologies, which include storage, transportation and market access, which have been showcased above already.

Company	Country	Details
Harvest CROO Robotics	USA	Harvesting robots for strawberry farms
Lineage Logistics	USA	Packaging, storing and transporting food using cold chains

Table 6.6. Well-known Start-ups in 'Post-Harvest'

4. **Soft-tech vs hard-tech:** This is another way to classify, although most models are a mix of all three: hardware, software and services. Many of the solutions offered are software as a service. Most technologies are just data analytics and software wrapped with a service around it, as far as the farmer is concerned. But there are increasing number of hardware-oriented technologies too which require actual devices to be used by the farmer on the farm. And even the most software-oriented or information-oriented tech will at least involve a smartphone! Lastly, most hard-tech solutions are also changing the ownership pattern to a lease, but it still involves some physical apparatus on the field. Let us look at this division.

   a. **Software-driven solutions:** The bulk of the farm advisory services as well as extension services or market access and information services (weather, price and acreage) are mainly data and software driven.

   b. **Hardware solutions:** Apart from the more customary tractors, irrigation and implements which are hard equipment, among newer technologies too, almost all the precision farming techniques involve some device or the other (sensors for below- or above-the-ground data); other optical readers, drones, robots and harvesting machines are all devices which become part of the physical infrastructure of the farmer (whether on shared, rented or outright purchased basis).

Company	Country	Details
Tevel	Israel	Autonomous flying fruit pickers—apples
DroneDeploy	USA	Map fields in minutes to conduct stand counts, identify variability and make in-field recommendations, all offline at the field's edge
FarmWise	USA	FarmWise Labs is a developer of farming robots designed to facilitate autonomous cultivation and organic farming; the company is developing the future of vegetable farming with machines which can adapt to different tasks to meet the needs of each farmer and each plant, at any time
ecoRobotix	Switzerland	Automated weed control robots; spray weed-killing chemicals precisely using 95 per cent less chemicals; solar powered and automatic, needing no supervision

Table 6.7. Well-known Start-ups in 'Hardware Solutions'

I also learnt from agritech investors like Omnivore another interesting way in which various business models in agritech can be looked at, based on whom the business primarily focus on: (a) farmer platforms for whom the farmer is the key, (b) B2B marketplaces which mainly provide solutions for businesses like a *kirana* store and (c) farmed consumer brands for whom the individual household consumer is the main focus. With all this slicing and dicing of this space, I believe that the reader should be able to understand which sub-segment any agribusiness falls under.

By now, you must have also understood how global and well-entrenched the supply ecosystem already is while adoption of these offerings by farmers is rising gradually. As we progress into the next few chapters, we will put the Indian agritech landscape into context. Less discussion on some agritech companies in this book is a deliberate effort because the book focuses on what the farmer can themselves use directly, and hence a lot of the very downstream or upstream areas have been mentioned only briefly.

PART IV

LAY OF THE LAND: A GLOBAL AND INDIAN PERSPECTIVE

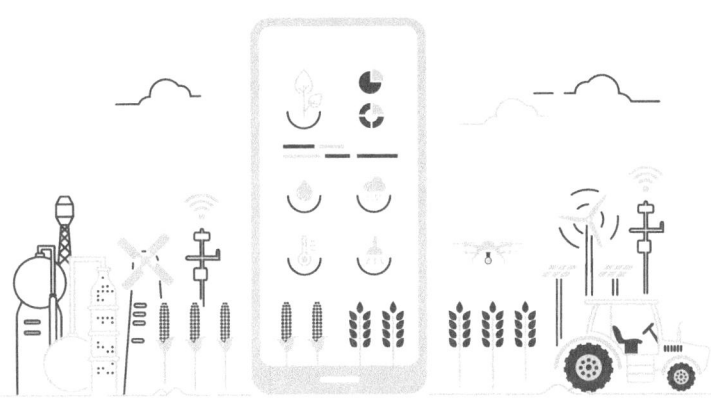

CHAPTER 7

MAPPING THE GLOBAL AGRITECH LANDSCAPE

Ground-up Story: Progressive Farmer

Jatin is a middle-aged farmer in his late 30s and runs his farms in Maharashtra. He has two brothers, and they all live together with their parents in a small village. The family owns about four acres of land between all of them, but they cultivate it together. He grows sugarcane on one acre and rotates jowar and soyabean on the others. He also takes short cycle crops like peanuts from time to time.

His 21 year-old nephew works in a large city nearby, his 19-year-old niece is studying in high school and his 12-year-old son is in the sixth grade. His son is curious about farming and accompanies him during the day and helps around where he can. He felt that his son might want to pursue a government job but could make double the money on the farm. But he also cited a social issue: To get them married and find a good family, a steady job was more acceptable than being a farmer. He also said that when his brothers and he retired, their children knew that they must be the ones taking care of the family farm.

I interviewed him over the phone as I was not able to visit that region. I shared with him all the different types of new technologies or modern methods which were available to them and checked his reaction. he was not aware of most of the things but found them powerful to adopt and was requesting me to send him more information so he could use it and even spread the work in his community. I talked to Jatin about AI-powered cloud and IoT-based sensor machines which he could use on a monthly fee basis, with the device being free to him. His first question was how it would be powered. He was very happy to learn that it would have solar batteries, and he would not have to worry about charging the device. He had heard about promotional schemes to sell chemicals and fertilizers but not of online marketplaces where he could buy his regular brand cheaper and get it delivered at the farm gate. To do that, he must travel 4–5 km to the nearest fertilizer and chemical shop and waste a full day. So a farm gate delivery with some discount on product price would be very welcome!

He had heard about apps such as Ola and Uber but did not know that similar apps exist for hiring tractors and equipment too. Currently, he used his phonebook contacts and word of mouth to hire from vendors who came recommended.

His voice changed when I mentioned FPOs and farmer cooperatives. This led to him sharing ideas with me. He thought that so much could be done if farmers could come together and have a meeting place, where they could subscribe to journals, share best practices and organize themselves for better prices and production techniques. They were already doing a bit of that when they needed to hire a truck to take their produce to the market, but not for any other thing.

Lastly, he was very open to hiring farm management service providers even on a profit-sharing basis and said that farmers would happily share the gains, if they make some extra profits. It would free up their time from constantly tracking and worrying about so many things.

While I wished him well and said my goodbyes, he reminded me to send him the video clip of the AI-powered sensor machine as well as the details of the online marketplace app, where he could sell his produce at a better price!

Clearly, the awareness about agritech has not really reached the farmers properly and when they hear about it, they are keen to learn, adopt and spread the good word around!

To understand the future of farming in India, and how our farms need to embrace modern methods and technologies to survive and thrive, it is imperative to first get a global perspective on this.

I have divided this mapping of the landscape geographically. There has been considerable progress made in countries and continents such as the USA, Latin America, Europe (+Israel), Africa, China and Australia. And each region has its own timeline on this and its own levels of success and impact. Technology and modern methods have been used in each geography in a different context or under varying compulsions, and it is instructive to hence look at this aspect too. It is also important to study the agritech landscape in various countries because the path taken by them may be quite different and hence throw up different insights.

Further, within each geography, I have tried to cover six aspects: (a) When did modernization of agriculture start off? (b) What was the catalyst? (c) How did the farmers adopt it? (d) What impact did it have on those regions? (e) What is the situation currently? (f) What lessons can be learnt from some of these experiences? In the below-mentioned framework, I have highlighted important and relevant aspects based on the availability of data of different countries.

THREE PHASES OF MODERN AGRICULTURE

If one looks at the timeline of progress in farming in general in high-income countries, there are three distinct phases.

The late 1800s to the mid-1900s was the 'first phase' where basic machines were adopted (tractors, irrigation, harvesters, etc.) and farmers shifted from animal to mechanical power. Single cropping, industrialization of farming and rising use of agro-chemicals, fertilizers and pesticides were the norm. The 'second phase' was in the late 1900s to the early 2000s, when environment consciousness and food security became important considerations, and the farmer had to shift their focus on maximizing production but minimizing impact on the environment. This led to the farmer adopting several modern methods and best practices. This included things like low input sustainable agriculture methods, no till, reducing usage of herbicides and fertilizers, organic farming, methods to prevent water run-off and leaching, crop selection to make it suit the agroclimatic conditions to optimize resources, better seeds, even some initial intensive farming like vertical and hydroponic cultivation, greenhouse systems as well as, to some extent, some precision farming and ZNCF. Since the last decade and a half or so, we have entered the third phase from the mid-2000s to the present moment, where technology is being used substantially in agriculture.

NEED OF A CATALYST

It will get amply evident as we go deeper into each region that there was often a clear and powerful catalyst which caused an upswing in the adoption curve of mechanization in the past and agritech in the current timeframe. One of such catalysts was the 'shortage or the high cost of labour', which forced farmers to be open-minded about adopting machines. Even today, farmers globally have a catalyst as they are facing pressure to 'increase their income and production' while 'reducing their environmental footprint' (soil, water pollution and land usage). This is forcing them to look at ways to increase production with lower costs. What better way to do that than look at tech? I also believe, at least in the not-so-rich agricultural economies, the very fact that the 'government fiscal situations' are tight, leaving them with little room to keep subsidizing farmers—farmers would be better off to look for solutions to make their farming sustainably lucrative, rather than keeping a lookout for government handouts. This should also be seen as a catalyst. A case in point seems to be Europe, where governments have supported the farmers extensively, and we see only early signs of tech adoption or innovation. It seems to be lagging some countries in Asia, for example, where the farmers are aware that the government can only do so much. 'Regulation' has also often been a powerful catalyst for change. The reason I wanted to briefly bring this up here is because this will form the basis of the pathways which are drawn up for policymakers and other stakeholders later on in the book.

EARLY DAYS THOUGH...

To also put things in perspective, agritech is at a very nascent stage globally. In the last decade, around 1,000 start-ups in agritech raised about $14 billion worldwide, while at the same time, about 18,000 companies in healthtech raised closed to $145 billion.[1] But the market is forecast to grow at a strong 18 per cent CAGR in the first half of this decade. We are already seeing that with some $30 billion being raised in 2020 alone.[2] The USA is the most advanced in terms of penetration and adoption of agritech on the farms, but Asia is likely to be the fastest growing, given the huge focus and investments likely to be made in China and India.

---

[1] World Economic Forum, *Innovation with a Purpose*.
[2] AgFunder, *AgFunder AgriFoodTech Investment Report* (2021), https://research.agfunder.com/2021/2021-agfunder-global-report.pdf

...BUT LOPSIDED

Another way to peel the onion is to look where agritech investments are going. To be clear, they have not been evenly spread across the spectrum. And this lopsided flow of funds will also need to be corrected even within countries which are attracting a lot of investments. Another study (EY report, September 2020) throws light on the last five years. Of the $6.5 billion of investments into agritech in the USA, $4 billion have gone into agribusiness (modern methods of cultivation) or farm management and precision farming, that is, on-the-field technologies and improvements. Only about $200 million have gone into market linkages. Even if you add up supply chain solutions as they are all post-harvest, it adds up to around $1 billion[3] (16% of total investments). On the flip side in India or even Asia more generally, so far, of the about $500 million which have been invested,[4] bulk of the investments have gone into market linkages and supply chain and almost nothing has gone into 'on-the-farm' technologies or upstream technologies. This is a very different path which VC and PE funds have taken in the USA or Europe vs how they are investing in this space in India or rest of Asia.

In addition, agritech can also be divided into upstream, midstream and downstream. Since the last five–six years, most of the investments have gone into downstream businesses, even though there has always been more scope for investments and impact in the upstream sector. Hence, it is very encouraging to see that in 2020, upstream investments overtook downstream for the first time in at least seven years. In summary, not only does the geographical landscape of agritech differ, but even the focus of those investments is quite different, and more evenness will have to occur in the near future to get the

---

[3] Tracxn, *AgriTech Sector Landscape Report* (August 2020), https://tracxn.com/d/reports-feed/agritech-sector-landscape-report

[4] EY, *Agritech towards Transforming Indian Agriculture* (August 2020).

maximum out of new technologies for the maximum number of people. Let me summarize a few key points seen in each of the major regions and countries in the world.

USA

The start of modern agriculture in the USA can be traced back to the late 19th century.

What Was the Catalyst?

This was catalysed by two main developments: establishment of (a) 'agriculture-focused universities' to impart specialized knowledge on cultivation and (b) 'extension centres' and the concept of imparting continuous training at the farm level. The need for higher produce led to larger area under cultivation and larger size of farms. This coupled with decreasing availability of 'farm labour' due to regulation or urbanization, the use of mechanization became necessary. That lead to the rapid inventions and adoption during the Industrial Revolution (the 1850s)—of tractors, combined harvesters, plough machines, reapers, and threshing and ginning machines. The USA has also been a pioneer in seed technology early on—primarily of hybrid seeds. Even irrigation began at the same time.

What Was the Impact?

The impact of all the above can be gauged by the immense increase in production. The USA was producing about 70 per cent of the world soybean production by the late 1960s, compared to just 3 per cent in the late 1930s. The second impact can be seen on the reduction of people employed and the increase in productivity. In the late 19th century, 64 per cent of the entire US population was engaged in agriculture. By the late 20th century, this came down to barely 2–3 per cent. During this period, the average size of the farm ballooned to

460 acres from about 200. Productivity also zoomed, as can be seen by the number of labour hours required to produce 100 bushels of corn. From about 35–40 hours in 1890, it dropped to just 2.75 hours in 1987. Table 7.1 below summarizes this transformation.

Year	Farmers in Labour Force (%)	Number of Farms (m)	Average Farm Size (Acres)	Labour Hours/ Bushel
1930	21.0	6.3	157	17.5
1940	18.0	6.1	175	12.0
1950	12.2	5.4	216	9.0
1960	8.3	3.7	303	5.0
1970	4.6	2.8	390	3.3
1980	3.4	2.4	426	2.8
1990	2.6	2.1	461	2.8

Table 7.1. US Trajectory of Modernizing of Agriculture over the Decades

Source: Mary Bellis, 'History of American Agriculture', ThoughtCo, 28 August 2020, thoughtco.com/history-of-american-agriculture-farm-machinery-4074385

It is hence natural that the USA would lead in the current wave of agritech and the next level of modernizing of agriculture as well. As per one US research firm, of the global top 50 agritech start-ups of 2019, 66 per cent were from the USA, 20 per cent from Europe and rest from Asia.[5] Looking at it in another way, as per the AgFunder 2021 report on investments, the USA had the lion's share of 51 per cent of the estimated ~$30 billion raised in 2020.

Lessons

One of the most important reasons for the early success of agritech in the USA can be attributed to the fact that there

[5] Hexgn.com

was a high level of 'literacy' among farmers and the desire to be 'progressive' driven by the need to improve incomes but also because they were convinced about the 'tangible benefits' from adopting technology. A light regulatory environment and high degree of liberalization in the agri-sector have also helped. The large size of farms and the homogeneity of crop within a cluster or belt have made certain agritech solutions like precision farming much easier to deploy and show results.

EUROPE

Europe overall is number 3 in terms of regions attracting investments into agritech, but it's driven primarily by the UK and Ireland. In recent times (2020), Europe has lagged the USA and China. While the USA and China saw a 30–60 per cent yoy increase in investments, Europe only saw a modest 5 per cent increase.

Italy

I am separating out Italy to drive a few points home. Like elsewhere, Italian agriculture also experienced major industrialization of farming when large companies started producing at mega scales to meet large export requirements. This left the small-to-medium farmer, who focused on single crops, out in the cold. They had two options: innovate or die. They, of course, chose the former. They left the vineyards and olive orchards to the big guys but found a way to maximize their 'boutique' farms.[6]

They realized that the only way to survive was to embrace excellence and differentiate themselves: grow the best tomato and best fruits in the world, use what was unique to them

---

[6] Università Bocconi's course material on 'Challenges of Agribusiness Management' course on Coursera.

(climate in the hill areas) and create a brand around their heritage or rustic fabric to monetize the pull of their region. This allowed them to differentiate and charge a premium for their produce. As they grew only in small quantities, it had the scarcity effect too. In an article, David Zaruk calls it 'becoming the Gucci of earth'. They went a step ahead and used the hillside beauty to also integrate agri-tourism. The results are for all to see. Not only did they survive, but the community is also now thriving.

Indian small farmers can learn something from this too. Most farmers are smallholders and may not get a lot of government support soon. These farmers would do well to try and play a similar premium, boutique and heritage game.

Another important driver of success in Italy was the young entrepreneur farmer entering the game with a fresh mind and flexibility. Today, 10 per cent of all farmers in Italy are below the age of 35, many of whom are women, and they are accelerating this success story further.

Apart from the Italian experience, in general, Europe seems to have lagged a bit behind some other high-income countries. David Zaruk, in fact, highlights in the same article reasons why agritech does not matter to Europe the way it does in the USA or Canada.[7] And this may well be an important fallout of regulation and subsidies which one must understand if one wants to allow agritech to flourish and benefit farmers.

Some very interesting start-ups in Europe across the spectrum include companies like Karma Foods in Stockholm, focusing on reducing waste at supermarkets. Anuland FieldSense is a precision agriculture company from Ireland using above- and below-the-ground data; Micron Agritech in Dublin has devised a way to test farm animals for parasites without veterinary

---

[7] https://european-seed.com/2019/02/ten-reasons-why-agritech-doesnt-matter-in-europe/

intervention and prevent an outbreak and save animals as well as farmer time;[8] and Gamaya in Switzerland is using hyperspectral imaging to help prevent pest and disease in plants.

ISRAEL

A mapping of the global agritech landscape will not be complete without a mention of Israel because Israel has been at the forefront of a lot of innovation in agriculture technology not only in the recent past but for many decades. No surprises therefore that Israel was the sixth largest country in 2020 globally to attract agritech investments—more than large agri-countries such as Australia and Brazil! Israel started its journey into agritech very early on, and due to its water scarcity, arid climate and shortage of land (half the land being covered by deserts), irrigation and precision farming have been natural focus areas for Israeli companies.[9] In fact, they were forced to innovate to survive. Netafim was started in one of the Kibbutz (community farming collectives), and Israel is today recognized as the inventor of the drip irrigation system used worldwide. Since its independence in 1948, agricultural production has grown sixteenfold! Israel has excelled in the areas of water management, soil improvements as well as new plant and seed growth.

With this rich background in agri-research and development (R&D), companies have been thriving with innovation across the spectrum of agricultural technologies. Over 500 companies operate in the field. Countries such as China, Africa and India are visiting Israel to learn and use their technologies and get inspiration.[10]

---

[8] Colm Gorey, *20 European Food and Agritech Start-ups Revolutionising What's on Your Plate* (January 2020), https://www.siliconrepublic.com/start-ups/food-agritech-start-ups-europe
[9] https://en.wikipedia.org/wiki/Agriculture_in_Israel
[10] https://www.agritecture.com/blog/2019/1/19/why-agtech-is-blooming-in-israel

Currently, companies such as Tevel (which use flying robots to pluck fruits like apples) and CropX (which use above- and below-the-ground data to reduce input consumption and increase yields) are two examples. Other interesting companies include Prospera, which focuses on yield prediction; Taranis, which predicts crop disease and prevents pest losses; and SuperMeat, which focused on plant-based meat.

ASIA

Asia can be seen in three parts: China, India and rest of Asia. China has been the second largest investment destination for agritech start-ups in 2020. Investments grew nearly 60 per cent yoy and accounted for about a fifth of all investments globally. Asia was number 2 in raising investments—China and India being the bulk of it, followed by about $334 million by Indonesia and $198 million by Singapore. Within Asia, I will just focus on China to provide the Asian context in the global landscape.

China

It is widely known and accepted that China is at the forefront and leading edge of agritech adoption. Even so, in January 2020, the government issued a plan (Digital Agriculture and Rural Area Development Plan 2019 to 2025) to further accelerate digital agriculture with specific numeric targets,[11] to nearly double the share of digital agriculture within overall agricultural value added to 15 per cent from about 7 per cent in 2018 and to increase to 15 per cent agricultural produce being sold online (from about 10% in 2018). The government is targeting a 70 per cent penetration of rural Internet connectivity and a fast 5G rollout as well. Robots

---

[11] https://www.foodingredientsfirst.com/news/chinas-agritech-acceleration-could-spell-dramatic-shifts-for-global-food-chains.html

and machines are being rapidly adopted in addition to new concepts of custom farming, farm adoption, creative agriculture, cloud farms and shared economy. These are no longer just buzz words.

But Chinese agriculture was not always so vibrant. Till the 1980s, agriculture and about 300 million people associated with it were strictly controlled by the state and Central governments. In the last 40 years, intensive agriculture has grown by leaps and bounds, and today about 25 per cent of the world's grain is produced by China, although it only has access to 10 per cent of the world's arable land.[12] In recent years, the government has placed even more focus on agriculture and rural development. The Twelfth and Thirteenth Five-Year Plans have focused on growing rural infrastructure, integrating environment-friendly practices in farming and consolidating farm labour into large, industrialized farms. In 2018, the government rolled out a plan to test innovation and technology in agriculture and measure its impact. This included robots and automated machines, AI and big data. Private sector also joined hands. Alibaba, in the same year, launched the ET Agricultural Brain to provide farmers with data and technology to improve their yields and profits.

By 2019, this test programme was operating in full swing. In certain provinces, one can today see drones flying above fields and driverless electric tractors and robots planting seeds in rows. With this level of automation and tech, a single person could run a farm where previously several hundred workers were required.

The catalyst for acceleration of modernizing agriculture in China was not very different than faced by many countries worldwide. Feeding the world's largest population and hence 'food security' is one key driver, but also as 'dietary patterns change' (more dairy, meat and proteins) and 'resources

[12] https://www.1421.consulting/2020/03/agricultural-industry-in-china/

like water get scarcer', it becomes important to 'protect the environment' and deal with climate change uncertainties. 'Food safety' has also been a very important issue for China, which it has increasingly addressed since 2015 and since China is a big agri-exporter, traceability technologies gain more importance. A large population and only a 'fraction of the world's arable land' imply resource scarcity. This has pushed agri-innovation on top of the government's agenda.[13]

There are several large private sector companies which are also leading this modernization drive apart from the government initiatives. Pinduoduo and Meicai are two more names other than Alibaba which are active in this space as well as a host of e-commerce companies which are supplying farm-to-fork e-groceries. In fact, Pinduoduo in September 2020 organized a nationwide competition to grow strawberries in the most efficient manner using tech.[14]

The Chinese agritech ecosystem includes companies like Meicai, which are online marketplaces to connect farmers to end consumers (B2B or B2C) as well as companies into organic farming and retail distribution (fully integrated) and companies providing the tools for high-tech farming like making drones.

LATIN AMERICA

As per the GSMA report on agritech landscape in Latin America,[15] a few interesting characteristics are worth noting. First, Latin America was found to be behind Asia and even Africa in digital tool availability and adoption. Second, it was

---

[13] Cindy Feng, *Exploring Agri-Food Tech Opportunities in China* (January 2018), https://www.startupbootcamp.org/blog/2018/01/exploring-agri-food-tech-opportunities-china/

[14] https://pandaily.com/china-aims-to-develop-smart-agriculture/

[15] https://www.gsma.com/mobilefordevelopment/wp-content/uploads/2020/11/Landscaping_the_agritech_ecosystem_for_smallholder_farmers_in_Latin_America_and_the_Caribbean_1.pdf

acknowledged that use of digital tools can have a very big impact on the income and earnings stability of the small-to-medium farmers. Third, most of the tools available were being offered by the government or NGOs with very little private sector or even impact investors involved.

Some of the catalysts seen in Latin America recently include the ongoing pandemic. Farms experienced an acceleration of digital adoption during 2020, as the pandemic made it more important to be connected and find new ways of increasing revenues or reducing cost. As face-to-face meetings were restricted, farmers were forced to embrace the digital world for information and transactions. Even the end consumer has used e-commerce to buy groceries and, in fact, farm to fork became a reality when small entrepreneurial farmers tied up with large gated residential communities to visit them two–three times a week and supply fresh produce. Freshness and less intermediary touch points as well as traceability became very important during the pandemic and have set this ball rolling. Sometimes, the nature of the produce and its exportability also determine tech adoption, as seen in China. For example, the coffee and cocoa value chains need traceability for exports and that has led to mushrooming of a lot of digital procurement solutions which provide record keeping and origin data.

Some of the key lessons: Multiple revenue streams are necessary for agritech start-ups to survive and thrive. Second, a private sector start-up ecosystem is critical for the next level of evolution, as purely NGOs or government departments can only kickstart the process but lack scalability. Another interesting finding has been that farmers are looking for holistic solutions. A patchwork of solutions is being offered world over, which needs simplification and integration to enable maximum adoption. Other learnings include importance of literacy, willingness to accept digital payments and cost of new tech and the need to deploy ready-to-use low-power wide area networks and connect IoT/drones/satellite data.

AUSTRALIA

Australia has followed the US timelines in adopting mechanization. The unique characteristic of Australian farming has been the 'average size of farms' there, which are in the thousands of hectares each. With that size, moving to mechanical machines and tools was imperative but also more viable, given the economies of scale. Australia has been quick to adopt environment-friendly practices like no- or low-till farming, as well as water management, to reduce ground soil or water getting infected. They now face problems of weeds which have become herbicide resistant and are focusing R&D efforts on that front as well. Agritech in Australia has therefore also focused a lot on precision farming to reduce the use of scarce resources.[16]

SOME CONCLUSIONS FROM THE GLOBAL LANDSCAPE

After outlining interesting facts and stories about most of the large countries in the world, I summarize some conclusions from the above.

- **USA:** The start of AUs and focus on more educated farmers led to farmer literacy and ability to see the value in embracing mechanization or technology. They had also seen the tangible benefits of the first wave of mechanization in a huge manner.

- **China:** A large population with changing dietary needs and shortage of resources has forced the government to focus on modernizing agriculture. Leading position in telecom and Internet technologies has laid a strong foundation for them to build rapidly on. A top-down push from the government, including micromanaging pilot projects, is a hallmark of the Chinese way.

---

[16] 'Discover Best Practice Farming for a Sustainable 2050', a course by the University of Western Australia on Coursera.

- **Israel:** Israel had huge scarcity of arable land and rain and hence had to strive to innovate to achieve near-self-dependence in agriculture. This led to its aggressive focus on R&D.
- **Australia:** Large size of farms allowed early adoption of mechanization. Problems with erosion of soil due to wind forced them to adopt better methods like no-till farming.
- **Italy:** Italy saw pressure from industrialized farms, which forced them to reinvent their product and positioning. Also, the entry of young entrepreneurs made a big difference in recent years (highlighted in Box 7.1). Europe, in general due to its strong farmer subsidy funding, has reduced the urgency at the farmers' end to make changes.
- **Latin America:** It shows the importance of a sustainable agritech supplier ecosystem, even while affordability at the small farmer level is low. It paints a picture of a fine balancing act, where with minimal creative pricing, private sector players must find a sustainable multipronged revenue model to survive and scale.

Box 7.1. Some Trends in Modern Farming by Young New Farmers in Italy[17]

Two notable aspects of Italian agriculture are as follows.

1. The first is how farmers in hilly areas have practised high-altitude farming and have become large centres of excellence. They have focused on 'boutique farming', that is, growing high-value crops in small quantities and combining it with tourism. Flat land agriculture

(continued)

---

[17] Course on 'Challenges of Agribusiness Management' by Università Bocconi available on Coursera.

(continued)

is commoditized, so mountain agriculture contributes more to excellence in products with more exotic and higher-value produce. They have also differentiated and branded their product by linking it to their geography. There is even a term for it: heroic agriculture.

2. The second aspect is how Italy has seen many young and new farmers entering the field. Almost 10 per cent of all farms in Italy today are run by dynamic creative energetic farmers below 35 years of age. Such farms are bigger in size and are displaying higher productivity than traditional farms. It is felt that new entrants into farming have no baggage of old views and customs and approach the business with fresh eyes. These new entrants are choosing sweet spots smartly after a lot of analysis, for example, avoiding industrial high-investment crops like wheat (where they can't compete with the giants) and crops like olive and grapes which have become an overcrowded space. Some other characteristics of this cohort of farmers is that 40 per cent of them are female. They have focused on 'servicizing' their offerings and using online and aggregation platforms to maximize their returns. For building engagement with their customers, they have used digital solutions and apps as well as run schemes like adopt a tree or farm. They are using scientific ways to track the growth of their crops. Collaboration with other farmers is very popular for various agricultural activities as well as information and knowledge sharing. Notably, a high rate of agritech adoption was made possible due to a lot of knowledge sharing and collaboration between farmers.

But agritech is just not about the start-ups. It includes a lot of other things. I have had the pleasure of participating in some very rich courses run by leading global AUs, and it will be instructive to highlight the kind of debates which are going on there and the best practices they are focusing on, which I do in Box 7.2 below.

Box 7.2. Best Practices in Global Agriculture

Some of the buzzwords used globally in academia as well as among policymakers are 'make farming profitable and protective' or 'double the produce at half the cost' or the concept of 'triple bottom line—for the farmer, society and environment'. This sums up almost all the key areas which are on top of the mind on this subject. It's about cost, yields, profits and protection. I am breaking these further into some smaller components.

1. **Nutrient management:** Techniques used for this include a balance budget, ways of reducing usage by keeping nutrients in the root zone and not losing it to wind, evaporation or ground water by leeching or run-off. Another concept used is of the 'right rate' because after a point, excess nitrogen is not used by the crop and actually reduces yield. It also ends up in ground water affecting farmers as well as the environment.

2. **Water management:** It includes sensitivity to the nutrient content which is going into water bodies. Other ways of reducing water usage practised are using plastic mulch and drip irrigation. In mulching, a thin layer of plastic with holes made to put seeds is used to cover the bed. This restores the sun rays for a longer time and retains humidity of the soil. It also restricts the growth of weeds around the main crop. Overextraction of water is prevented by using plastic pipes to drain excess water. Ditches, canals and roadbed catchments are made to save water. Larger farms use centre pivot irrigation systems, which are very efficient and prevent leeching of water below the root zone. Contour-planting is another practice in sloped farms to conserve water by making furrows, tracks and rows, so that water and even soil do not evaporate or run down.

3. **Soil conservation/conservation tilling and soil testing:** Topsoil is the most important asset a farmer has. It is what gives them productivity and income. Hence, protecting

(continued)

(continued)

and preserving that is of utmost importance. Soil structure improves water retention, hence needs attention. Rotation of crops and between farm and pastures helps conserve the soil productivity and enhance it. In fact, coupled with use of different herbicides, it also reduces negative impacts of low or no tillage.

4. **Climate related:** Flexible farming is an interesting concept focusing on adapting to climate change and dealing with increasingly erratic weather. Such changes will force farmers to adapt sturdier crops or rotate crop more often based on weather forecast. Further flexibility in land use could be to use land for dairy farming or poultry farming more if their systems are more flexible. Also, they may own or lease land in different climate zones as a risk management strategy. Even the aspect of changing the timing and speed of sowing operations is to be considered. Raised bed farming is another technique which is not only environment-friendly but also helps in almost all the above areas.[18] Its primary characteristic includes higher yields due to longer planting season, lower weed growth and conserving rainwater, leading to better pest management.

5. **Others:** The best practice for smallholding farmers being practised even in India by some, to increase cultivable area, is to put up wired boundary walls around the farm and grow creepers.

Note: Inputs from courses run by the University of Florida; University of Illinois Urbana-Champaign; Università Bocconi, Italy; and University of South Wales, Australia.

---

[18] https://www.agrifarming.in/commercial-raised-bed-farming-a-full-guide

A TECHNOLOGY MAP IN SUMMARY

I wanted to summarize the scope and spectrum of technologies which are currently being deployed globally in terms of hard machines and soft technologies to conclude this chapter. Broadly speaking, while the full spectrum is wider, most of the action in agritech has been in these two key clusters.

1. **Smart farming:** This includes using machines, robots, data, AI, IoT, satellite, machine vision, machine learning, drones, sensors and cloud computing for actual farming activities such as sowing, harvesting, irrigation systems, weeding, crop choice, lowering costs, sorting, packing as well as blockchain for tracking produce. Using data to refine cheaper lending and insurance solutions has also been an active area.

2. **Marketplaces:** This includes connecting the farmer to vendors and customers and reducing intermediaries to improve farmer economics, including the use of appropriate storage solutions as needed.

And the primary objective of all these has been to increase the produce (food security) and improve farmer profitability while keeping agriculture sustainable (environment-friendly even while climate changes).

I will draw upon many of these learnings in the next few chapters as I bring it all together.

CHAPTER 8

THE INDIAN AGRITECH LANDSCAPE

Ground-up Story: 'You Mean It's Already Happening?' 'I'll Just Google It' and Other Stories

I had the chance to interact with a very senior NGO founder who has been doing grassroot and livelihood work in villages of Gujarat, Rajasthan and Madhya Pradesh for nearly 30 years. One of the most important learnings I got from the meeting was about the progressive things that the governments at the Centre and various states have already been doing for the last few decades. Short courses for farmers' children in agritech areas was one, awards run by the government to motivate progressive farmers was another and very good work being done by some KVKs was a third. 'You mean it's already happening?' was my reaction. I felt like I was dreaming! Agritech training and rewards—perfect combination! 'And that too, all these schemes and programmes have been there for 10–20 years,' he told me.

I will add here another very interesting story which sums up the supply and demand mood quite well.

I was walking down a steep terraced apple orchard in Himachal Pradesh, when I saw a young girl grazing her family cow. What caught my attention though was that she had a book in one hand. I stopped to ask her if she was studying, to which she sweetly answered that she was doing both at the same time! She was studying in 10th grade and had her national competitive exams coming up in a few weeks! But she also knew basics of farming and helped around when she could. On my way back up, I crossed the farmer's house and started asking the farmer's wife some questions. She was very excited to hear about flying machines which can pluck their apples and sensors which can read above- and below-the-ground data and help them reduce cost and improve yield. She had not heard of any of them and wished it was available to her. She was not even aware of platforms where she could buy or sell goods at better prices, nor was she aware of so many government schemes which could benefit her. She had joined many Facebook groups which promised to be information-sharing platforms, but she got nothing from them. She would love to have an advisory service and pay for it. She felt that using IoT sensor devices was worth it, if benefits could be demonstrated. A few hundred dollars a year in charges was affordable. She was keen that her two daughters study modern agriculture methods during their college or even through online apps. She felt that farming could change a lot if new methods, best practices and online technologies are adopted, and she was looking forward to it. She already saw a lot of potential and opportunities, but her only problem was farm help. Her husband had a side business and was away from home most of the time. Her two daughters were studying. That just left her to do a lot of the farm-related work. She strongly felt that if tech could reduce the manual nature of farming via machines and online solutions, the kids would find it more attractive to stick to it, as manual hard work was one of the bugbears which kept the kids away. Before I could take my leave, she had quietly asked her daughter to make some tea for me. I told her that she should not have disturbed her daughter while she was studying, but their hospitality was so heart-warming. I found the tea very sweet (even for my liking!), and she promptly offered to make me another. I asked her to let her daughter do well in her exams and I would come back for a less sweet tea next time! While I walked away, I noticed that her daughter was busy on her smartphone.

When I asked her what she was doing, she said that she was googling the names of agritech companies I had just mentioned to them!

This was the other side, where farmers were not having access to many of the information of local schemes but were very progressive. I really felt that the awareness deficit must also be frustrating for the people who knew of all the good schemes but didn't see them reach all the farmers. This gap must be bridged!

Now that we have a fair understanding of the global landscape of agritech and how the value chain is defined and divided, a good sense of the kind of companies and solutions as well as their global availability, it is appropriate to assess the situation in India.

This chapter will trace the history of what is available already in India for the farmer in terms of machines, technology as well as new business models. It will elaborate which parts of the value chain the solutions are mostly focused on, how they currently propose to solve the problem and what it means for the farmer in terms of investment or change.

TRACING THE ROOTS OF AGRITECH IN INDIA

At the outset, it is informative to revisit and sum up some salient features of Indian farming to better appreciate the paradigm that exists. There are six main characteristics of Indian farming: (a) its small and marginal farmers, (b) low literacy levels in rural India,[1] with about 73 per cent vs 88 per cent in urban India, (c) low income of about ₹10,000 per

---

[1] Government of India, *Household Social Consumption on Education in India*, NSS 75th Round (July 2017–June 2018), http://mospi.nic.in/sites/default/files/publication_reports/Report_585_75th_round_Education_final_1507_0.pdf

month as of FY2019,[2] (d) poor dissemination of information, knowledge, training and advise, (e) cheap and abundant labour has meant low urgency to mechanize and (f) lack of easy financing. These have been the primary causes for the low mechanization and technology adoption in India in the past. But some of that is changing, and this change must accelerate in the future to ensure that agritech adoption is high and benefits come through.

WHAT DO WE HAVE?

I will sum up the current situation in three key buckets.

Mechanization

The best way to gauge the level of mechanization in the country is to look at the tractor penetration. That is the first step in mechanization, as further equipment and advancements get fixed onto a tractor. Another way is to look at power consumed at the farm level. A report by the Indian Council of Food and Agriculture (ICFA) estimated that as of FY2014, the overall mechanization rate in Indian agriculture was about 45 per cent.[3] This was low vs the 57 per cent seen in China and 75 per cent in Brazil—other lower-middle income countries with large agriculture base. This has grown at a steady but quite a pedestrian rate as seen by the increase of power consumption to 2 kwh/hectare in FY2014 vs ~1.5 kwh/hectare in FY2006. Even this 45 per cent hides the stark polarization between segments—where only harvesting and threshing processes have a higher 65 per cent mechanization rate, while all the rest (irrigation, seeding, planting, weed removal, etc.) have a very

---

[2] https://www.hindustantimes.com/india-news/rs-6-000-is-6-of-a-small-farmer-s-annual-income-according-to-nsso-data/story-rddMw0hk6cSbxjo7E1GyKK.html

[3] https://www.icfa.org.in/assets/doc/reports/IFMM.pdf

low 30–40 per cent rate. However, the dropping supply of farm labour and their rising wages are increasing the pressure to adopt more mechanization. The huge impact on productivity, yields and costs and consequently on the farmer's income remains the key driver of further increases in mechanization. As overall demand increases, it will broaden the demand for more diverse mechanized equipment such as threshers, rotavators, reapers, power weeders and transplanters, rather than just tractors and power tillers, which has been the case so far.

As per the latest information available, India has an installed base of about 5 million tractors.[4] Based on total arable area of about 156.4 million hectares,[5] this works out to a penetration of 1.5 hp/ha. The developed country average is about 8–10 hp/ha. So clearly, with more affordability, awareness and marketing of tractor-mounted solutions, this penetration can grow. One must also keep in mind that government support and grants play an important role in helping this demand and hence will have to continue. In fact, since many of the new technologies are tractor mounted (sensors, spraying equipment, harvesting and even no-till equipment), higher tractor penetration is going to be a prerequisite. Another rising phenomenon is of renting tractors by small farmers, and hence penetration data may be understating the actual 'use' data. Recently set up CHCs by the GoI aim to accelerate this process by renting out tractors and farm equipment to farmers. We can look at the penetration data in a few other ways. Given that the average size of farm holding in India is about 1.08 hectare, this means that there are about 144.8 million farms in India. A 5–6 million tractor base means that there is one tractor for every 30 farms. And the fact that there are 650,000

---

[4] https://www.business-standard.com/article/pti-stories/itoty-2019-india-s-first-awards-show-for-tractors-and-farm-implements-119050700194_1.html
[5] https://www.macrotrends.net/countries/IND/india/arable-land

villages in India, and India sells about a million tractors a year,[6] it means that about 1.5 tractors are purchased per village every year! All these go to establish the fact that the starting point of mechanization is indeed very low, but readers should not assume that a low base will automatically lead to higher demand. It should hence not lead to complacency because basic mechanization is a building block to further digital farming. At the same time, to reduce the risk, stakeholders—government, entrepreneurs and farmers—should also keep a focus on technologies which do not presume the presence of a tractor (electric scooter-based tools).

New Technology

It is hard to get any kind of penetration data on new technology in farming because it is still a nascent industry in India. Let's try to triangulate and get a sense. One way would be to measure the total investment going into this field. As per Inc42, a research portal focused on new technologies, cumulatively till 2019, all Indian agritech companies put together (there are over 500 start-ups already) had raised only about $500 million of equity investments. In 2020 itself, the industry raised about $136 million. As per AgFunder, this figure stands at a much higher $1.8 billion (half of it was Zomato itself—which is not agritech in the strict sense of the word) though. Globally, agritech companies raised about $30 in 2020 (a growth of ~35% over 2019). That gives India a ~5 per cent share of the global pie. Another way—and probably a better way—to look at it is the current size of the agritech market in terms of revenues of the players involved. An EY report in September 2020 (*Agritech: Towards Transforming Indian Agriculture*) estimated the size to be just about $200 million vs a total opportunity of $25 billion, That's a fraction

---

[6] https://www.tmaindia.in/consolidated-monthly-reports-2021.php

(less than 1%) of the opportunity. But probably the best way to look at penetration is by the number of farmers already touched by agritech in one way or another. Again, proper estimates are hard to come by, but given the fact that most agritech companies are focused on B2B solutions, directly active farmer numbers which are available with various sources (largest agritech company websites) talk about 25,000–500,000 farmers at a maximum per company with an average of about 100,000. Even if we assume that about 150 companies are focusing on farmers directly, that is 15 million farmers. On a base of about 150 million farmers, it's about 10 per cent of farmers.

Inc42 estimates[7] that the agritech ecosystem in India is already tapping less than 20 per cent of farmers—about 30 million. I believe that this is a very generous estimate.

Another way to look at it is penetration of the eNAM service which has been active for about five years now. As of 2019, there were 16–17 million farmers on that network (11%), but my research shows that active ones may be much lesser. eNAM is part of agritech and one of the larger pan-India, government-initiated platform and a good proxy for gauging adoption. So every way that we may look at it, the penetration is between 1 and 17 million (1%–11% of the base).

New Farming Business Models, Methods and Best Practices

This is probably the most difficult aspect to estimate but based on the above data, one can say that it will also be a very small portion. The way I define new business models is to include farmers who may not have mechanized their farm, nor using sensors or robots, but have adopted modern

---

[7] https://inc42.com/infocus/startup-watchlist-2021/startup-watchlist-8-indian-agritech-startups-to-watch-out-for-in-2021/

agricultural practices and scientific best practices to improve their earnings. This will include becoming a part of an FPO, actively engaging with KVKs for continuous improvement at the farm or leasing in land to get benefits of scale. In Chapter 2, I have mentioned that about 14 per cent of arable land is under leasing. FPO membership across the 10,000 odd FPOs is (average size would be 1000 at best) about 10 million farmers as a most optimistic estimate. Even this number is just 5–6 per cent of the total farmer base. One can also gauge the extent of best practice adoption with the number of extension service agents available who are actively engaged with farmers to enable them to learn the best practices. As highlighted in the research paper[8]—published in April 2019 in the *Research Journal of Agricultural Sciences* (RJAS)—the number of extension service agents in India is far less than the recommended 1 per 750 farmers. Even so, they are often kept busy in non-extension work. India only spends 0.7 per cent of its agricultural GDP on R&D and education (which include extension services), while the Word Bank recommended level is 2 per cent. Often the agents are not up to date on the latest developments in technology globally or best practices followed. They also need regular refresher training. Of the about 145,000 total extension officer positions available by the Central government, only about 90,000 are filled. Rest of the positions are lying vacant. This has kept the ratio to 1 officer for every 1,162 farms vs 1 for 750 guideline set by the government itself.

Figure 8.1 sums up the situation and the point India is at. For the purposes of this figure, the farmer base has been taken at 150 million and assumed current size of 10,000 FPOs with about 1,000 members each. All data is not for 2020 and is as updated as available.

---

[8] Ravi Nandi and N. Swamikannu, 'Agriculture Extension System in India: A Meta-analysis', *Research Journal of Agricultural Sciences* 10, no. 3 (April 2019): 473–479.

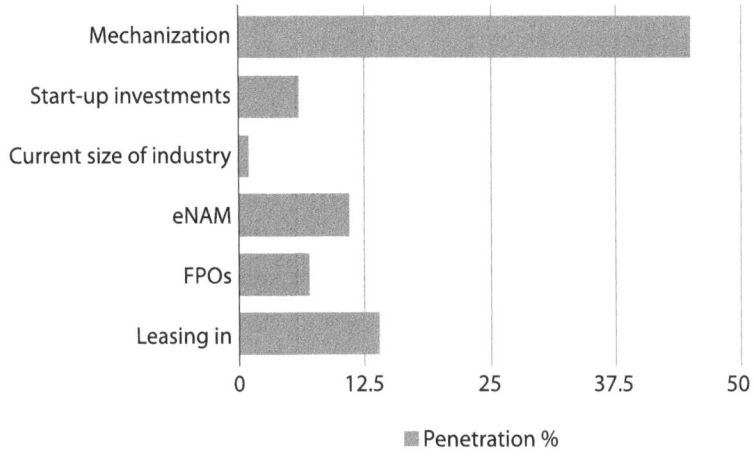

Figure 8.1. Current Penetration of Modern Systems

Source: Included in Footnotes 3–8 and in the text above.

Without spending too much time on this, I would like to suffice by saying that I have tried to establish the fact that Indian agriculture and farmers are at an extremely nascent stage in the adoption cycle of mechanization, agritech, best practices or other modern methods or business models. And it is in this context that I will outline the current landscape of what is available across the spectrum. But I also want to highlight some success stories that already exist. Box 8.1 captures some of these.

> **Box 8.1. Success Stories Exist and Must Be Highlighted Repeatedly**
>
> 1. **Sita Devi and Her Capsicum Greenhouse Farming**[9]
>
>   Sita Devi was from a farmer family and based in Lucknow. Even though both her sons had left farming and lived in the USA, when she fell alone, she thought of restarting farming. She thought of growing capsicums. On the advice of her son, she also explored greenhouse cultivation. Soon the enterprise started flourishing and now she exports her produce.
>
> *(continued)*

---

[9] Based on author's interviews.

(continued)

2. **Jitendra Patidar and Ambi Wines**[10]

   A young boy from Ratlam, Madhya Pradesh, the only graduate in his village, realized that his father was growing table grape crops at their farm and went to Pune to do a master's diploma in wine-making technology. He also went to California to learn wine-making in more detail and now runs a successful vineyard and wine business.

3. **Vimal Chavda and VNR Seed**[11]

   It is probably one of the biggest success stories which have been undermarketed in India (other than in some agri-bureaucracy/NGO circles). This is the story of Vimal Chavda from Raipur, Chhattisgarh. Vimal's grandfather was an agriculturist and expert and had a farm of about 3 acres in the 1950s. His father went on to do a PhD in agriculture-related topics, and Vimal entered the field with a master's from an AU. Early on, he focused on drip irrigation techniques in the 1990s, visited Israel, got new technologies, practised farming at an industrial scale and got in drones and big machines from the USA. He even sent his kids to leading global AUs to do their master's. He has set up housing, education and health infrastructure for all his farm labour. He runs contract farming in a big way and also a large seeds business. Today, he probably operates farms of more than 10,000 acres.

4. **Sahyadri Farms: A Successful FPC**

   Sahyadri Farms[12] is an example of a hugely successful story in the FPC space. But it is an FPC with a difference. It is a privately started enterprise with a good amount of seed capital. It does not depend on the grants and financial

---

[10] https://www.hindustantimes.com/indore/vintners-put-village-in-madhya-pradesh-on-global-wine-map/story-jX2hV8sN569DXBT1LOHlaK.html
[11] Based on author's interviews.
[12] www.sahyadrifarms.com

> support of the SFAC and hence has scaled up very well and has access to the best management resources and skills. It was started by a farmer from Nashik area, Vilas Shinde, in 2000 to explore the idea of CF. From 2004, it started exporting grapes to Europe. It expanded this till 2010 with about 150 marginal farmers working together. By 2014, it had grown to 1,000 farmers in the FPC. It then moved into aggregate input buying, drip irrigation and poly houses for indoor agriculture. It recently also tied up with agri-advisory firms to receive advice. Today, it has several fruit- and vegetable-processing infrastructure and exports most of its produce. It has also installed all the modern technologies and equipment on its farms, including their own weather stations. They have a large cold storage facility as well and use blockchain technology for traceability. When I mention Sahyadri to other FPO managers or NGOs, they are very impressed with it and emphasize what good management and some financial support can do. We need more such Sahyadri Farms!

CHARACTERISTICS OF THE LANDSCAPE

After a detailed study of the existing landscape, certain characteristics of the current progress of agritech companies become evident.

1. **Very concentrated start-ups:** The first and foremost aspect to understand is which parts of the chain are most of the Indian agritech start-ups present in. There are about 500 start-ups in India already, and they are present across the spectrum, but the large ones have focused on either the marketplace model (to buy or sell) for inputs and to sell the produce or on precision farming. There is a small cluster of companies in financial services which is using data to reduce underwriting risk on insurance and loans and offers it to farmers at a lower price. Other areas which

have some players are biotechnology (seeds) and renting services (for tractors and equipment). We barely see companies in the machinery and robotics manufacturing or even in farm infrastructure (greenhouses and indoor farming). Even within the two large segments, the largest cluster is that of marketplaces/output linkages, having raised about 60 per cent of all funds raised by the industry last year. This concentration is notable.

2. **Institutional or export focus:** Another evident characteristic of the Indian agritech space is the high focus on B2B or international markets. My research has shown that actually many of the companies operating in the marketplace space have a B2B focus because it is easy to sell to a few institutions vs millions of farmers, and there is no affordability issue. Many large start-ups are also focusing on the exports market where profitability can be high. In a sense, it is the low-hanging fruit which does not need grassroots-level footprint or need to charge the farmer who may not be able to afford it.

3. **The product and service offered:** Within the marketplace business, some companies provide the platform to the farmer but get paid by the input seller (large companies) or the institutional buyers (retail chains and restaurants). Bulk of their volumes are usually B2B, with a small fraction coming from actual farmer selling on them. Even that reach to the farmer is via FPOs or through local agents appointed by them. Even so, the farmer has begun to benefit from lower costs and somewhat higher price realizations. If they can get cheaper inputs (along with some unbiased free advice) and ability to sell directly at the farm gate to an institutional buyer and do away with the *mandi* system, they are going to realize more and get paid promptly and with a fair grading and weighing of their produce. One challenge in certain rural areas is delivery of the input to the farm. If service providers can

ensure delivery at the farm gate, the farmer adoption will be very rapid. Some may be following a hybrid model, where the farmer orders online at a cheaper rate but needs to pick up from a nearby collection point. Often, despite tall claims by many companies which they have a farmer-based model, they may be procuring from the *mandis*. Hence, the farmers may not be seeing benefits yet.

The precision farming companies usually are selling a packaged bundle of solutions, where they would have a hardware device which would be planted at the farm and assist in collecting data via sensors. On top of this, using satellite images, more data would be captured on a continuous basis about weather, soil, pests, nutrients, etc., historically and currently. After analysing that data, advise would be given on optimum crop selection as well as input selection to increase the yield and reduce the cost. Usually, this advice is given via a smartphone app on a real-time basis via a phone call or even SMS. Most of these companies have gone to the farmer directly, avoiding the FPO route. But even within this segment, a B2B route exists where the large buying corporate is paying for their services as the buyer benefits from the better quality of produce on farms they buy from. This is the path of 'assurance farming'.

WHAT DO THE NEW AGRITECH OFFERINGS MEAN FOR THE FARMER

- **Investment:** In the input and output marketplace model, the farmer does not have to spend or invest anything. It is a low touch model for them, experimental with no skin in the game. They can try it out; if they do not benefit, they can go back to buying and selling on their old ways. In the precision farming/smart farming space though, the farmer is the payer, as they are buying a service. Usually, there is an investment to buy some hardware (sensor and laptop) and a subscription service for the data crunching and analytics and access to the cloud data. But usually, the monetary commitment is quite low, benefits are quite tangible and payback is usually in less than a year. Some models are already converting to a total FaaS model, where the hardware is for free, and only subscription is charged. This reduces the entry friction. The monthly subscription can be as low as $20 a month. And a farmer can see a much bigger payback within months. But the more important part is the commitment of effort, which I address below.

- **Change of ways:** Some of the agritech solutions may not demand a lot of financial commitment but a lot of mental and emotional commitment in a sense that the farmer is required to change their ways, do their job in a different way and listen to an outsider with no 'earned' credibility on advice about their ways of working. But even this is not a very big issue, as they can adopt on a piecemeal basis and once the benefits are visible, they can roll it out across their fields. But they must be willing to try new things. Either grow different crops or grow them in a different variety. Use more machinery for tilling, weed removal and harvesting. This calls for a big change, and hence can still take a long time to convince. My research has shown that even at the individual farmer level, both ability and willingness to pay exist—all they want to see is a sustainable, tangible benefit to their own bottom line. The other more challenging change needed is computer literacy and ability to operate a computer and applications, input some data and read out some outputs and instructions. Some of this is solved by mobile apps in vernacular languages, but heavier farm management software may need laptop-based access. But again, most farmer families have sons or daughters who are well educated and are spending quite much of their free time, helping with the farming activities anyway and should be able to help. In fact, this could excite them and reignite the interest in 'smart farming'.

In Box 8.2 I list down some startups across segments.

> **Box 8.2. Some Indian Companies in This Field Based on Their Area of Primary/Initial Focus**
>
> **Input Marketplace**
>
> There are several companies in India in this space. Many of them offer multiple services across the horizontals. But I classify them here based on their primary core offering.
>
> **Bijak:** It is an online marketplace for purchase of inputs and sale of output. The company is operating in 28 states and covers 100+ commodities. It provides an app-based service with in-app payments and helps farmers with working capital financing, so that they can make on-time payment to the seller.
>
> **DeHaat:** It is an integrated total solutions company which serves about 500,000 farmers across 8 states. It provides online marketplace for buying and selling for the farmer as well as advisory services to the farmer, soil testing, farm analytics, etc.
>
> **BigHaat:** It calls itself an online agri-store and focuses on being a marketplace for all inputs which farmers need, including machinery, equipment and tools.
>
> **EM3:** It is a FaaS company, currently based in Uttar Pradesh, Madhya Pradesh and Rajasthan. It provides core farming services through mechanization as a pay-per-use (rental) basis, including land preparation, sowing, crop management, harvesting and post-harvest handling. It sends itsown trained and qualified staff to do these operations for the farmer.
>
> **Tringo:** It is a company promoted by the Mahindra Group and focuses on renting out tractors and other farm equipment to farmers.

(continued)

(continued)

Precision Farming Horizontal: Companies Using Data Analytics and Devices to Improve On-farm Efficiency

CropIn: Started in 2010, the company focuses on using data from the farm as well as on weather, and helps farm produce buyers or lenders as well as farmers in better decision-making. It also offers inventory storage solutions, and using micro data helps lenders and insurers take better decisions. It also provides traceability for buyers and focuses more on the institutional buyers as their customers.

Fasal: Fasal is a company started in 2018, focusing on horticulture, providing inputs to farmers for smart farming, lowering input costs, irrigation efficiency management, predicting disease/pest attacks via its sensor-based hardware which is fixed on the farm and satellite-based 14-day weather information as well. It also includes a farm finances management solution to help the farmer keep track of their cashflows and expenses. It is currently covering 7–8 states and about 25,000 acres of land. It prices its product at ₹30,000, with a monthly subscription of ₹400–₹600.

FarmERP: It is a farm management software company, and its application also provides weather forecasting and yield forecasting capability. It is more broadly focused on agribusinesses in general, rather than just the farmer as an end customer.

Stellapps: This company is focused on the dairy vertical and uses smart farming inputs for efficiency across the dairy farming activity. It is specializing in digitizing the entire dairy supply chain. The scope includes cattle monitoring, milk procurement and cold chain management. Its solution includes a wearable IoT device plus an app. It also offers cheaper insurance packages and helps in reducing veterinary costs and improves milk yield.

Intello Labs: This is a PHL management company which digitizes all quality info of fruits and vegetables for growers, packers, wholesalers, exporters and retailers. It also provides traceability information.

Traceability

SourceTrace: It enables both farmers and buyers with transparency and traceability using its technology platform which helps replace cumbersome manual record-keeping which was also low on credibility.

Agricx: This company serves the large buyers and traders/wholesalers to assess quality of their produce using just a camera phone and their mobile app. It also uses spectral technologies to give lab-like results based on images of the produce.

Output Linkages/Supply Chain

Ninjacart: Currently operating in seven large cities of India, Ninjacart is a pure supply chain company. It buys fresh fruits and vegetables from farmers as well as *mandis* and sells directly to retailers. It uses farmer harvesting schedule data, demand trends and spot market prices to procure and deliver produce on time and at efficient prices. The logistics is managed with technology to reduce wastage and to do it faster.

WayCool: This company operates end-to-end supply chain logistics, supplying food items to hotels, restaurants and general stores by buying directly from the farmer. It currently handles 350+ tons of food products per day, across 18,900 clients, and from a network of 50,000+ farmers in more than 50 regions in India. Its products include staples such as rice, pulses, wheat flour, dairy and value-added products. It does pre-planting to harvesting advisory for farmers and gets into contracts with farmers and ensures 100 per cent offtake.

(continued)

(continued)

Crofarm: This Gurugram-based company functions across fruits, vegetables and grains space. It ensures higher-than-*mandi* prices to farmers and provides demand insights to help farmer grow the right thing and harvest at the right time. The company provides the buyers within 12-hour fresh food. The farmer gets payments promptly and digitally. They work with 10,000 farmers currently and handle 60–70 tons of food per day and serve about 5,000+ buyers.

Agribazaar: This is an online marketplace connecting farmers to buyers through an app. It includes digital payments, financing and warehousing solutions to smoothen the logistics process. It also has an input purchase feature now and does quality testing through its app as well as offline. It is also offering advisory to farmers.

Ecozen: It is a Pune-based company, being over a decade in the business. It has three main areas of operation. Its core flagship product is the solar-powered cold storage solution which can be installed on the farm or collection/distribution point. It also sells a solar-powered pump for irrigation and, lastly, it also operates a marketplace connecting farmers with buyers. It mainly focuses on fruits, vegetables and flowers.

Ergos: The company has built several warehouses of its own across Bihar and eastern Uttar Pradesh. It goes door-to-door and collects farmers' produce, providing them with electronic warehouse receipts and financing against it. Its revenue model is to charge the buyers and non-bank financial institutions (NBFCs).

Fintech

Samunnati: This is a Chennai-based NBFC which is focusing on helping FPOs with input-buying, output-selling advisory and support. It also provides farming technology and cropping advisory and finally ties this all up with loans to farmers for inputs and equipment as well as to finance the output sale.

There are other companies like payAgri as well.

Farm Machinery

Terracroft: It is a Manipal-based maker of farm robots called KrishiBOT. The tractor-like battery operated and self-driven vehicle perform a few key farming activities, including sowing of the seed, applying fertilizer and even weed removal. It does the work of almost 30 farmers. The company provides both buy and lease options.

FlyBird: It is a Bengaluru-based company started in 2013, which makes irrigation controllers and related equipment. It helps reduce irrigation costs and improve yield.

Urban Farming

Barton Breeze: It started out as a company operating hydroponic farms and has grown to provide consultancy and build hydroponic as well as greenhouse farms for others too.

Urban Kisan: It is a Bengaluru-based hydroponics farm, growing vegetables and greens and supplying fresh food to the cities.

THE MISSING PIECES

Having a close look at the global spread of technologies and comparing that with what is available in India, we can identify some promising 'white spaces' where Indian start-ups are absent, and hence new start-ups can target and global companies need to be pursued to bring their solutions here by partnering with local entities. Some of these spaces are as follows.

1. Mechanized and automated harvesting and robotic machinery space, which has companies from the USA,

Switzerland, Spain and Israel, is mostly missing. These companies make crop-specific harvesters for vineyards, apples, strawberries and machines for weed control (without using pesticides).

2. Even-pesticide-spraying technologies used by mounting sprayers on the tractors, which are super-efficient in reducing pesticide usage and wastage, have not been focused on.

3. The area of reducing PHLs, either by enhancing the shelf life of the produce itself (company like Apeel) or by building cold chain transportation and storage infrastructure (lineage logistics), is a space still not taken up in a big way.

4. Controlled environment agriculture as a whole is a space we see with a few hyper-local companies only. Indoor vertical farming, greenhouse farming, hydroponics and aquaponics are quite big in the USA and Europe but haven't seen that much traction in India yet.

5. Farmer-to-farmer resource- and knowledge-sharing networks are almost absent as well (FBN and Wefarm) and could be a good opportunity to tap and slowly build farmer trust and team spirit, which could be a precursor to closer collaboration via FPOs or CF eventually.

6. Within at-the-farm technologies, globally and even in India, there is almost no company offering total solutions for maximizing number of crops which can be taken in a year for rainfed farms. There are technologies needed for that to dry the moist produce and prepare the land to enable sowing the third or fourth crop.

With this understanding of the Indian agritech landscape and 'supply' from a business perspective, we will move to assessing the government policy landscape.

CHAPTER 9

WHAT THE GOVERNMENT IS DOING AND WHERE IT SHOULD FOCUS

Ground-up Story: Faith and Optimism

During my extensive travels, I had the chance to interact with some government and quasi-government bodies and academics as well. It was important to get their perspective on this whole subject but more importantly to understand from them how to look at the various government initiatives in this area. One of the extension services office heads surprised me with his positivity and case studies of success stories of how the government is engaging with farmers on the field as well as through workshops held at their centres regularly once or twice a month. He outlined how not only the farmers were curious and proactive in approaching them but also how the policies were effective, and farmers were getting large grants for modern equipment and tools to use on the farm, and they were all aware and using these schemes. A senior farmer I met in another state echoed this and said that he was aware and a beneficiary of various schemes and that he remained open to adopt more change and was always assessing and evaluating new ideas which he heard from government experts. An NGO head replied, '700 is more than enough, no shortage at all' to my question if there were enough KVKs in India. He went on to say that KVKs were also staffed with high-quality people with the appropriate qualification and experience and that it was all 'great on paper'. Another senior academic that I spoke to said that there was a lot of change coming to Indian agriculture and eNAM, FPOs, KVKs as well as the host of agritech start-ups show that India is in front of this trend. A very large farmer I met told me, 'I spent 2 weeks on a training camp about soil testing at the KVK and since then, my fertilizer consumption is down by 50 per cent!' A senior KVK official summed this up when he said, 'If not for the very large government machinery in this sector, left to just private sector, the agri-sector would have been in a far worse condition.'

I thought that the feedback and tone from senior operatives and academicians in the agri-economy were for the most part very encouraging and spoke volumes of the work being done but also of the optimism and faith people had in the system. But I was also curious to understand what one of the experts meant by 'on paper'. It is in this light that I move to the this chapter which focuses on exactly this—what has been the policy support and approach on this and what more can be done.

This chapter outlines how the GoI has looked at mechanization, agritech and modernizing agriculture over the years. What has been done in terms of policy support and reform to facilitate availability and adoption of such? Whether it is financing the farmer, opening centres to allow renting of equipment or the multitude of schemes to financially support new entrepreneurs in agriculture modernization (warehousing, processing, etc.)? It also includes some ideas based on global experiences, where the government can change the policy thrust or make it easier for adoption of the existing policies.

POLICY CONTEXT

It would be fair to say that one thing no one can blame the government for is to have over the years launched and operationalized a multitude of initiatives, institutions and policies to address the various moving parts of the agriculture value chain, with respect to modern methods of farming. Indeed, as one studies the topic deeper and interacts with the various stakeholders, you realize, sometimes to your surprise, that there is a set-up for almost everything you can think of! This has been done by different ministries and wings of the government over time and has created a very large, complex mesh of policies, schemes, institutions and agencies, so many that it is often difficult even for the insiders and seasoned sector experts to navigate through. But the point is also that there is a lot that exists already.

Let's start with the basics—focus on small and marginal farmers: SFAC, which was started under the Ministry of Agriculture in 1994 to focus on implementing government schemes for inclusion of small farmers. Schemes like eNAM as well as the whole FPO initiative are spearheaded by SFAC. On-farm mechanization and a push into irrigation have been made by the government since Independence and accelerated in the 1990s, and today nearly 50 per cent of all arable land is under irrigation—much more than the world average of only 20–24 per cent. Similarly, the tractor-manufacturing industry in India has been nurtured and encouraged right from Independence to have a dozen manufacturers who are not only today the largest tractor makers in the world but also the largest exporters. The government has also set up Central AUs (CAUs) and state AUs (SAUs) to impart high-level education and conduct R&D. These universities in turn collaborate with other research institutions and organizations to conduct ongoing research on innovation in agriculture. They have also set up (as discussed in Chapter 4 in more detail) KVKs in the 1970s to take this lab knowledge to the farms. Under the Ministry of Agriculture, there also exist extension centres across the country to impart further business knowledge and advisory on cultivation to farmers on an ongoing basis. More recently, availability of financing and insurance has also been taken up to ensure that farmers have access to pre- and post-harvest credit as well as crop insurance. The onset of Aadhaar, a nationwide identification system, and bank account opening through the financial inclusion drive has ensured that a lot of financial benefits to farmers (NREGA or PM Kisan) can be remitted directly, avoiding leakages and misuse. The setting up of a 'Doubling the Farmers' Income' mission a few years back is another example of policy thrust continuing in this area. Apart from this, there are multiple research bodies in India such as the ICAR, MANAGE, Indian Council for Research on International Economic Relations (ICRIER) and Indian Chamber of Food and Agriculture (ICFA), which are running various research programmes across the spectrum of agriculture. NITI Aayog has its own agriculture expertise and that also acts as a think tank with proposals and long-term strategic thinking in this area. Another agency is the Agriculture Technology Management Agency (ATMA), whose role is to help capture and extract micro data which farmers can use. This is done using simplified technologies and even in absence of Internet or smartphones. The National Academy of Agricultural Research Management (NAARM) and National Mission on Oilseeds and Oil Palm (NMOOP) are two more bodies. NMOOP, for example, is focused on increasing irrigated land for oilseeds and encouraging best practices like intercropping to increase overall yields. The GoI has also introduced the PM Sinchai Yojana (irrigation scheme) which encourages and funds increasing irrigated land and use of advanced irrigation technologies for conserving water on the farm. It is reported that the government has committed nearly $8 billion for this. The PM Paramparagat Yojana (focused on encouraging organic farming) is another scheme which is active.

To increase mechanization, the government provides grants and subsidies for the purchase of tractors and equipment, conducts demonstrations to explain the benefits as well as trains people for the repair and maintenance of such equipment. The Farm Machinery Training and Testing Institutes at Madhya

Pradesh, Haryana, Andhra Pradesh and Assam established by the government are playing a vital role in this.

The CAUs and SAUs in India are very important pieces of the solution. It is a resource which should not be underutilized or ignored. Hence, I have devoted some more space to this aspect in Box 9.1.

> **Box 9.1. AUs in India: Key Part of the Solution**
>
> There were a total of 70 AUs in India as of January 2021.[1] They are divided into three parts: Central, state and deemed universities. ICAR is the main governing body of AUs in India. Almost all states have at least one such university, except Arunachal, Goa, Meghalaya, Mizoram, Nagaland, Sikkim and Tripura. But only two union territories (Delhi and Jammu & Kashmir) have an AU, though there are many more universities which provide agricultural education.[2] The primary focus of these universities is teaching, research and extension services. Uttar Pradesh took the lead post Independence to set up US-style land-grant universities (I have discussed this briefly in Chapter 7 as to how this was a big catalyst that put the US farmer on the path of modernization) post a report by S. Radhakrishnan, and after inviting a US team and visiting the USA as well, in 1960, under the monitoring of the University of Illinois, the G. B. Pant University was set up in Pantnagar (now in Uttarakhand). Agriculture (including education) is a state subject in India and hence SAUs are the main component of the 70 AUs (54 are SAUs). ICAR even set up a model Act for AUs to standardize AUs' curriculum and way of teaching. SAUs have been based on the US-four-year system with semesters and GPA-based continuous grading. There is a trend, however, of SAUs now even demanding to
>
> *(continued)*

---

[1] https://en.wikipedia.org/wiki/List_of_agricultural_universities_in_India
[2] https://en.wikipedia.org/wiki/Agricultural_Universities_(India)

(continued)

> be converted to CAUs. (There are five CAUs in India, the one in Bihar being the latest to be set up/upgraded in 2015–2016.) The motivation for this is, of course, shortage of funds to pay for research or even pay pensions to its retirees. (And Punjab AU, which many years ago asked for this status change, is the top ranked AU in India today.) Overall, as of FY2013, there were about 67,000 students enrolled across all AUs in India. The staff strength, however, was about 50–60 per cent on average of the approved posts available.[3]
>
> Such a large network of high-quality institutions, spread well across the country, is the backbone of advancing and modernizing agriculture in India. These should not be underutilized. They need to be well funded, attract more farmers' children and offer short in-person and even online courses for students who cannot join a three- or four-year-course and as a refresher to update on newer agri-trends being practised globally.

REFORMS GALORE

In addition to the policy thrust, reforms in the agriculture space in India have also been an ongoing story. Although it may seem to have received less attention vs industrial reforms because agri-reforms may not have been as big bang as India saw in terms of trade liberalization in the 1990s, every few years some or the other reform has taken place. In the last two decades alone, we have seen several major steps being taken. Starting from a 'model APMC Act' in 2003, to the APMC reform (via eNAM) and 'warehousing reforms' under WDRA Act in 2007, after which the NCML entities were set up under NCDEX for better risk management by farmers in the mid-2010s to the 'land lease laws' model agreements drawn by the Centre in 2016, reforms and policy change have touched all aspects of farming so that farming could be modernized

[3] http://www.iauaindia.org/introduction.htm

with equipment and more efficiency could be built into the value chain. In fact, even before that, in the early 2010s, the programme to get fibre and Internet access to all 650,000 villages (BharatNet) was launched. It is indisputable that this is the backbone of all new technology adoption in farming. The focus on inclusion (universal service obligation [USO]) even in telecom spectrum and license award ensured that telcos rolled out their network in rural areas too. This has enabled farmers to access information on their handphones today. In 2018–2019, the government 'reformed the procurement of produce' by expanding the scope of crops under it—which in turn would reduce the concentration of crop selection by farmers and lead to better and more scientific farming practices. Even the way to calculate the MSP was made more profitable for the farmer during that time. Around the same time, the government also focused on encouraging new business models by establishing CHCs through which small farmers could hire latest equipment and use in the farm. More recently, in 2020 itself, we have seen the somewhat controversial move by the government to introduce some 'big bang' reforms by opening the marketing and sale channel for the farmers (APMC deregulation), streamlining rules around 'contract farming' as well easing on 'storage rules' under the Essential Commodities Act. Again, the thrust on increasing the number of FPOs and companies so that small holder farmers can organize themselves to improve their buying and selling power as well as share best practices, raise funds, create brands and do value-added processing of their produce is another big step to help the farmer in modernizing. Collectively, all these have set up the ground for progress towards modern farming, best practices and adoption of technology. One can debate whether we have enough KVKs or extension officers or whether they are properly funded (and we will dwell into that later), but the fact that various building blocks are available and ready to use is a good place to start with and shows that the government is supportive about modernizing this sector.

Table 9.1 summarizes the major policy and reform initiatives taken by the government and currently in force and which aspect of the value chain they address.

No.	Initiative/Agency	Issue Addressed
1	KVK	Centres under the AUs or ICAR: to disseminate technology developments
2	NREGA	Rural unemployment scheme
3	PM Kisan	Famer cash payout scheme
4	ICAR	Main body under which all AUs are organized; main research body
5	MANAGE	Extension services
6	ICRIER	Research institute
7	ICFA	Think tank; resource centre to promote food and agri-sector
8	Agricultural Technology Management Agency	Focused on spreading new technology to farmers
9	NAARM	Academy of research management; training institute under ICAR
10	NMOOP	Promoting modern methods in the oil seeds area
11	Farm Machinery Training and Testing Institute	Focused on training and technical help on farm machinery
12	AUs	Education and research on agriculture
13	BharatNet	Fibre network into rural India
14	Model APMC Act	Reforming the *mandi* system
15	Model Contract Farming Act	Reforming the contract farming rules
16	Model Land Lease Agreement	Reforming the rules around leasing of land for farming
17	CHCs	Enabling renting of farm equipment for small farmers
18	WDMA/NCML	Helping storage and financing of produce and risk management
19	FPOs	Collective bargaining and activities to enjoy scale benefits

No.	Initiative/Agency	Issue Addressed
20	eNAM	Better price discovery on national basis
21	ACABC	Engaging rural youth in agri-related vocational training and activities
22	PM Sinchai Yojana	Promoting irrigation
23	PM Paramparagat Yojana	Promoting organic farming
24	SFAC	Implementing schemes to ensure small farmers get benefits of policy
25	Agri Investment Fund	Promoting rural infrastructure on storage, processing and enabling even non-farmers to set up
26	KCC	Pre-harvest financing based on landholding
27	ARYA/MAAYA	Motivating, attracting and retaining youth in agriculture

Table 9.1. Summary of Various Government Policies, Institutions, Agencies and Schemes

The eNAM and contract farming are very important parts of the current mix of the Indian agritech landscape, and I have expanded on them in Boxes 9.2 and 9.3.

Box 9.2. Electronic National Agricultural Market

eNAM is the government's answer to address the output market linkage requirements of farmers. To unshackle the farmer from restricted local *mandi* access and to enable them to freely access markets across the country to sell all their produce at the best possible price, eNAM was launched in April 2016. It also addresses issues of transparency and efficient and prompt payments. Currently, about 175 commodities are available on the platform to trade.[4] Across 21 states and UTs, 1,000 markets are on the platform. Four states of Madhya Pradesh, Maharashtra, Uttar Pradesh and Rajasthan account

(continued)

---

[4] enam.go.in

(continued)

for nearly half of these *mandis*. Of the 140–150 million farmers in India as of February 2021, about 17 million farmers were on the platform. This is a big improvement over the last few years, where only 25 commodities were traded and only 4–5 million farmers were on it. In FY2022, the government plans to further increase the coverage to another 1,000 *mandis* to bring total coverage to 2,000 (out of about 6,000–8,000 *mandis* in India). FPOs are also integrated into the platform and can trade on it. About 1,800 FPOs (out of ~10,000) are already on the platform.[5] Total trading volume on eNAM has crossed about ₹1.22 lakh crore in FY2021, nearly double of the ₹59,000 crore in FY2019. As some of the pressure points of better IT connectivity, infra and more awareness picks up, this is a very promising platform which should be embraced by farmers and FPOs in a bigger way.

Box 9.3. Contract Farming[6]

Contract farming is a very potent solution to the major problem that small farmers face—that of reliable consistent market access for their produce at a predetermined fair price. It also includes a lot of extension advice by the sponsor and use of modern methods and technology which helps reduce costs and increase yield. Although ITC first set up such an arrangement in the 1920s, there was not much activity till the 1960s when some seed companies started contracting farmers. This kicked off only in 1989 when PepsiCo contracted Punjab farmers for tomato procurement and then for potatoes. Long discussions with several senior NGOs running hundreds of FPOs (lakhs of farmers) highlight

---

[5] http://www.businessworld.in/article/Decoding-e-NAM-Catalyst-to-Digital-Transformation-of-Mandi-System/09-02-2021-375678/

[6] https://www.longdom.org/open-access/contract-farming-a-boon-to-farmers-2329-888X.1000124.pdf; https://indianexpress.com/article/explained/why-govt-brought-new-act-in-2020-despite-having-legislated-a-model-contract-farming-law-in-2018-7187807/

offtake as the biggest problem. Even most online grocery B2B companies apparently end up procuring 90 per cent from *mandis*, rather than from direct farmers. Hence, a long-term contract farming model can be very helpful. The large basmati rice companies have been doing this for years (KRBL: India Gate brand; and LT Foods: Daawat brand), but given the lack of legal clarity, despite nurturing the crop, they had to bid for it in the *mandi* only, till recently. The Punjab Contract Farming Act was passed in 2013, and formal activities under this were being carried out. Based on this, many other states had enacted their own local laws as well, making it legal. In 2018, the GoI framed a model Act on contract farming. And in 2020, this was superseded by a new law which had some changes (land leasing, disputes, etc.). Hence, contract farming can be a very positive catalyst, once mechanism is put in place to prevent or mitigate risk of exploitation or corruption at the sponsor's level. I highlight contract farming in this chapter as it is one key route to modernizing agriculture and increasing use of technology and something for which laws and a framework also do exist. This does not mean that the contract farming system is free of all risks. Exploitation risk via low price fixation can occur, and strong dispute resolution mechanism and punishment must be there. Confusion about risk of contracting farmer losing right over their land has to be cleared up.

OTHER STEPS TO FACILITATE ADOPTION

Over and above the policy history and ongoing reforms, there are some other initiatives taken by the government to address the last-mile adoption by the farmer. These are worth highlighting as I wrap up the 'supply' landscape.

1. **Financing help:** To overcome affordability problems faced by the farmer, in the long run, higher income is the best solution, and a host of things are being done for that,

but in the near term, availability of easy and affordable finance to be able to invest in modernizing their farms is very important. The government mainly addresses this via not only KCCs but also DBTs. Recently, the government has launched the Agri Infrastructure Fund to infuse equity and government-guaranteed loans at cheap rates for projects implemented by farmers or new entrepreneurs to fund farming infrastructure. This is a useful move.

2. **CHC kind of initiatives:** Another way to address affordability issues is to encourage the shared economy and allow farmers access to the latest technology on a rental basis, keeping the friction low and giving easy access. The CHCs is one such move, which will help farmers. This should be accompanied by after-sales service and repair support. One of the AUs in Bihar is actually starting a one-year diploma course in just training mechanics for farm machinery. This is a commendable move and must be replicated by other AUs and even private institutes.

3. **New entrepreneur support for modernization:** Recently, given the overall vibrancy in the agriculture ecosystem and rising interest of urban adults to pursue agriculture-related activities and careers, the government has looked to tap into this talent pool by making new farmers or agri-entrepreneurs eligible for many of the benefits available to the traditional farming community. New farming professionals may enter select areas of farming value chain (storage, smart farming and urban farming) and hence may need more targeted incentives for them to get more involved and invest knowledge and financial capital into agricultural activity and bring about faster modernization. The Ministry of Agriculture & Farmers Welfare in December 2017 launched the grand agriculture challenge in collaboration with Startup India, where start-ups were invited to submit tech solutions for several critical problems. Winners get three months of

handholding via experts. This is a very smart and timely move.[7]

4. **Facilitating knowledge sharing:** The ministry also has set up a 'farmer portal' which has exhaustive and updated information on all aspects of farming from inputs to cropping patterns right down to your state and block levels. It is a great resource and available across languages. It also allows for receiving text alerts on various things which the farmer can choose. This is a very good tool to encourage farmers to adopt best practices by making knowledge available so easily.

5. **Vocational training:** Another very interesting scheme run by the government is the ACABC, where it ties up with NGOs or grassroot entities to provide a 45-day in-house (residential) course and training on vocational agri-related courses. Once they complete this certificate course, they are eligible to apply to the government for loans up to ₹20 lakh to start an agri-related new business. Most of the students which come are farmers' children. The only prerequisite is that they have to be a minimum 12th grade graduates (with two years of agri-related specialization at high school or junior college level). The courses offered include areas such as goat farming, poultry, dairy farming, agri-sorting and packaging. An NGO I spoke to which runs one of these runs 2 batches of 35 students each in a day and has demand for this from even bachelor's and master's students of agriculture who want to take vocational training in this field. This scheme can be made more effective if post course and financing the ventures are monitored as ground research shows that many of them shut down after a pretty short period. A farmer in Gujarat did not know about these and requested me to send him information for his children.

---

[7] http://nmoop.gov.in/conference/docs/Background_Paper_Agri_Startups.pdf

A PEEK INTO HOW AND WHAT GOVERNMENTS AND MULTILATERAL AGENCIES GLOBALLY HAVE DONE TO NURTURE THIS SPACE

It is worth looking at what various governments or multilateral organizations have been doing to promote modernizing of agriculture. For example, the UN World Food Programme in Munich in 2016 started an innovation accelerator programme offering funding solutions, experts access and reach to global companies. The WEF started the New Vision for Agriculture initiative as well. While the Indian government and state governments are focusing on similar things, I would like to highlight it, as there may be opportunities to identify gaps and do more.

In general, governments have been focusing primarily on creating an ecosystem to allow start-ups and innovation to thrive, providing financial assistance and incentives, helping in securing and attracting talent as well as advising on scaling up avenues. Equally important support has been in the form of ensuring a robust telecom infrastructure and aggressive education campaigns to help change consumer/farmer behaviour. It has been noted that most times it's just about (a) education and (b) helping the farmer financially to get over the short-term economic challenge of adopting such environment-friendly and modern processes.

WHAT NEEDS TO BE DONE: SOME SUGGESTIONS AND IDEAS

It is very clear from the above points that the policy and reforms and steps being taken to accelerate adoption by the old and new farmers are all a very good basis and starting point. It is also clear that the frameworks have been well-laid-down, and the ecosystem is well-entrenched. Recent momentum also shows how things are moving very much in the right direction. The government gets it and is moving at a good pace towards a much more vibrant, robust and modern, efficient agri-economy.

Having outlined all this, it is also important to however not get carried away with the above alphabet soup. Two conclusions of a recent article by Invest India (a government body for promoting investments into India) sum up my point very well: (a) that too many entities are involved in altering parts of the value chain and (b) in absolute terms, very little has been done and a lot more needs to be addressed.

Some Key Suggestions and Ideas

1. **Umbrella body:** As I mentioned above, there are multiple bodies under various government departments which are engaged in a host of initiatives, schemes and programmes. There is an urgent need to rationalize them. Just as the government started rationalizing all its rural development policies a few years ago, I would suggest the same for schemes meant for modernizing agribusiness. In fact, I would go one step further and suggest that an umbrella body be formed and rationalized initiatives to be placed under that one umbrella organization. For example, currently, KVKs and the extension office have some overlap and are run by different departments. It would serve us well, if they were in some way brought together under one roof. The unified umbrella body would have a holistic solution looking at all aspects of agritech, modern farming, new business models, best practices, automation, mechanization, etc.

2. **Clear goals:** This umbrella body should be given clear quantifiable goals. For example,[8] China in January 2020 released the 'Digital Agriculture and Rural Area

---

[8] https://www.foodingredientsfirst.com/news/chinas-agritech-acceleration-could-spell-dramatic-shifts-for-global-food-chains.html

Development Plan 2019 to 2025'. The government-led initiative establishes hard targets on the value of digital agriculture (15%), online sale of agri-products (15%) as well as rural Internet access (70%). The percentage of farmers using a laptop or desktop, for example, is also a metric tracked and used by the US Department of Agriculture. Such clearly stated numerical goals could help make even current diffused efforts more impactful. Clearly stated, well-defined and quantified goals with a glide path are always easier to monitor, implement and achieve. The government should lay out its vision and definition of modernizing agriculture by whatever name it wants to call it—digital, tech-driven or something else— and define the scope, goals and how it is going to measure the success.

3. **Staffing:** The government must increase its knowledge-sharing infrastructure (number of centres and staff) and spend more on their training. There is also a need to motivate and incentivize the staff through meritocratic goals and targets. Proper performance assessment and pay will go a long way in weeding out the flab and making these teams lean but motivated, self-starters rather than pen pushers who are just occupying the position. Contract assignments like the ones used for teachers in many public schools could be one way to keep the teams more engaged and proactive. Even so, 90 per cent of a KVK's budget is spent on just employee cost, leaving almost nothing to carry on experiment, research work or do field trials for new tech which they are approached with. Hence, overall budgets need to be increased once an accountable performance assessment (based on outcomes) can be put in place. Current KVK performance assessment is based more on inputs (what they did). From this, it should give due weightage to what the farmer did (outcome) as well. Did they adopt it? And what tangible benefit did they draw from it?

4. **Tie-ups and a global perspective:** There are many countries from which we can learn and many private sector companies globally which are having a lot of experience in this area. The government, through this umbrella body, should collaborate with them so that such expertise can be used in India. The focus of KVKs or extension offices also needs to change. Much greater focus needs to be included on the best practices and new technologies and business models being adopted in other countries. Many of them may be very doable in Indian conditions too. I quote here from the article on Chinese agritech by Benjamin Ferrer to drive my point home: 'I think the biggest hindrance to the Agri-tech boom in China is the lack of Chinese people traveling abroad to learn more about new practices. They need to bring in more outside experts to improve their strategy.' This is exactly what I mean that needs to be done in India too.

5. **Risk aversion:** As mentioned previously in the book, farmers tend to get dependent on government support if it is excessive and constant and seen as a backstop. It affects not only their farming decisions but also hunger for growth and risk appetite to experiment. We need to stop this if we want a farmer ready to take advantage of all the new tech developments. It can be done over 5–10 years and with a glide path shared in advance to help the farmers prepare for it. The European example shows that incentive for farmers to modernize is low if they expect continued government subsidies and support. Also, the Latin American experience has shown that if just the government is active in this space, they will struggle to find scale.

6. **Recognition:** Incentivizing farmers to adopt tech is important. The government could launch contests for the most digitized farm in every village or district and give them six—nine months to show their results. Awards

could be ₹1 lakh per winner, and these could be conducted within each extension officer's radius of villages (100,000 clusters with 1 winner from each). The government will have to spend only ₹10 billion, but it would lead to millions of farmers embracing tech each year. Currently, some state governments do have some reward programmes. A farmer in Madhya Pradesh told me that he won the first prize in a contest focusing on yield improvement by correct input usage and for motivating others. Maybe the time has come to launch a national contest focused on agritech and advertise winners nationally. This will also help spread it by word of mouth.

7. **Start-ups:** The government has been supporting start-ups in agritech. However, there are some suggestions for taking it further. The government could fast-track and help the start-ups navigate through local laws and regulations which govern farming practices. It could also get their solutions to be tested in the central labs and, once approved by them, give them direct access to all the KVKs and extension offices to promote that technology aggressively. Currently, these extension teams only promote technologies which the university labs have approved. Lastly, government could open agritech parks where start-ups could get demo fields allocated to showcase latest tech at grassroots level. Financing support to farmers to adopt agritech solutions will see quick payback for the government too (e.g., saving in fertilizer subsidy bill). In short, as some agritech start-ups and investors put it, be an enabler and identify and correct any bottlenecks in the regulatory environment.

8. **Pandemic, a catalyst itself:** Many countries have seen that the last 12–15 months of the COVID-19 pandemic and the resultant disruption to supply chains and mobility have led to an accelerated take-up of digital solutions. The government should also increase its facilitation activities

so that agritech can have a bigger impact in providing lasting solutions to some of the disruption.

9. **Two-way flow:** The government must see itself as a supporter of agritech as well as a user to collect farm- and farmer-level information, inputs on policy design, data on policy awareness, implementation as well as outcomes. It should focus on maximizing the benefits and minimizing the negatives of agritech. A recent World Bank report echoes this point as well.[9]

The government also continues with its efforts. Just in June 2021, the government had released a consultation paper for an India AgriStack.[10] Under that, it is proposing to set up a National Mission on Digital Agriculture, which will be governed by an advisory council, comprising all stakeholders, which will have a three-year implementation plan. The building blocks will also include modules on farmer unique ID and service interface as well as weather information, commodity prices, government schemes, geospatial farm-level information, and a complete digitization of the lab to farm offering, to be used by KVKs, AUs and extension officers. It is a step in the right direction. This will energize the start-up ecosystem and reduce a lot of the duplicate effort each one must do to set up the services as well as to onboard farmers.

This perspective of the history and efforts made by the government to modernize agriculture as well as a flavour of where other governments have focused I lay the ground to now get into the heart of the matter—how much is the farmer aware and what do they think about modernizing and using technology.

---

[9] https://openknowledge.worldbank.org/handle/10986/35216
[10] https://agricoop.nic.in/sites/default/files/IDEA%20Concept%20Paper_mod31052021_2.pdf

PART V

GROUND STORIES AND FARMER INPUTS

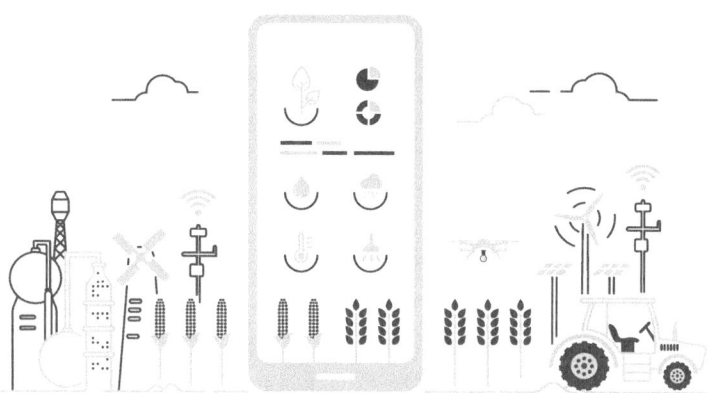

CHAPTER 10

WHAT THE FARMER KNOWS AND THINKS

Ground-up Story: Understanding the Nuances Is Key

It was nice of Suresh* who was a partner at one of the largest rural market research and consulting companies in India to help me get in touch with one of the senior-most grassroots-level farming professionals in the country. Mr Himesh, who is based in a village in Rajasthan, was happy to share his insights and views. On a rainy night in Mumbai in early 2021 monsoon season, I settled down to have a chat with him. He had been living in villages in deep rural India since 1994 and heads an NGO as well as oversees a KVK in his area and several FPOs too. When we got talking about how receptive farmers are to new ideas on farming and whether they are sceptical about urban folks coming to them with business ideas in agritech, he very strongly reacted saying that in his 30 years of living in rural India, he had never heard the term 'trust deficit' or 'sceptical' being used for farmers. To his mind, these are very misleading comments. The farmer is very simple and pure; if you ask them what they want, they will tell you. Don't have an agenda and don't try to navigate them towards your objectives. Just ask them, and they will tell you the way it is. But they do take time to share with you their thought process. And for that, he said that you have to spend time with them and understand their motivations, fears and frustrations as well as their hopes and optimism and their history. Understanding those nuances are key to finding solutions which will work for them!

Note: *Name changed.

FIRST-HAND DISCUSSIONS WITH FARMERS ACROSS INDIA

Designing solutions for farmers requires a lot of inputs from them. Globally, many start-ups have failed due to lack of adequate inputs from the farmer. I am sure that there are such cases in India too or will emerge soon. In fact, there is a full report by CTA (Technical Centre for Agricultural and Rural Cooperation) which only focuses on reasons for such failure[1] and is a must-read. That is the reason why a very large part of my book deals with actual farmer interactions.

Although the book is sprinkled with takeaways from farmer interactions in each chapter, this chapter consolidates all the insights I got from about a hundred such meetings on a broad spectrum of topics. Farmers from all across the country have been interviewed, covering states such as Bihar, Chhattisgarh, Madhya Pradesh, Rajasthan, Kerala, Karnataka, Telangana, Gujarat, Maharashtra, Uttar Pradesh, Haryana, Uttarakhand, Himachal Pradesh and even Jammu & Kashmir. The selection of farmers also included very small and marginal farmers with less than 2 hectare land ownership to the very large farmers owning over 100 hectares, from very traditional farmers who are old school to the very progressive ones who are well on their way to digital farming, from farmers growing horticultural products up in the mountains to the small vegetable farmer on the outskirts of large cities. I have tried to make it as representative as possible and believe that a broad spectrum

---

[1] Shepherd, *Lessons for Sustainability*. (Wageningen: Technical Centre for Agricultural and Rural Cooperation ACP-EU [CTA], 2016).

of farmers has been covered over the last year. Apart from cultivators, I have also interviewed various key stakeholders who are involved at a grassroots level. This list includes think tanks, BDOs, extension officers, NGOs, consultancies, FPOs, KVKs, agribusiness companies, agritech start-ups and agritech investors as well. I have incorporated all these insights together in this chapter with respect to understanding and presenting the farmers' thought process.

One interesting feature I have noticed is that the answers you get for the same questions differ a lot as you move from one kind of farmer to the other. I realized that there were four kinds of farmers I ended up talking to:

1. Small or very small holder, growing for self with little surplus, old with children not in farming
2. Medium size holder but unaware
3. Medium size holder with young members involved, somewhat aware and more progressive
4. Large holder, young members involved, high level of awareness and very proactive

It would be useful to the reader to keep this in mind to get a context of the insights shared below and also to understand how the answers can change quite a bit if a farmer crosses over from one to the other category.

1. **Low focus:** Many of the small holding farmers have struggled with their 'hand-to-mouth' situation for very long and have already taken up jobs and reduced their dependence on farming a while ago. Or they have kept their land fallow or given it on lease to others. Such farming families have, hence, a very low focus on exploring new approaches to farming.

2. **No serious thought:** Some have heard about new developments and possibilities but are so tied up in their

day-to-day struggle that they have not given it any serious thought. Such farmers continue to do what they know without changing. But these are also the ones who with a little push could embrace new methods.

3. **Not for them:** Others have heard of various changes taking place which are accessible but feel that it is not for them as they are very small farmers or they are old school and less flexible and think that such changes will not really help them and won't work. This group would need more effort in converting.

4. **What's there to learn:** Then there is this interesting group of farmers (and there are quite a few of them) who feel that they are already doing this for so many decades and know whatever there is to learn about cultivation techniques. Some large farmers have said that they pass by the KVK 'model' farms and are convinced that their crops are healthier. Another one said that at one KVK, the staff was asking them about certain practices they were following. While I had the opportunity to attend a course on 'Sustainable Agricultural Land Management' at the University of Florida, I was surprised to hear a professor say, 'It is difficult to convince them that there is a problem.' And he was talking of a farmer in the USA. Another course professor said that 25 years of experience has shown that it is very difficult to give advice to a farmer about their farm which is better than their own knowledge and decisions. It needs a lot of very micro-level information which outsiders will rarely have. At best, you can give ideas for them to consider—a very key thing to understand. This shows that the challenge to make farmers adopt more modern methods is felt everywhere, and we should prepare for it systematically.

5. **Do not want private sector involvement:** Farmers generally are wary of anything 'private' coming into agriculture. This is because of years of propaganda

that private sector can only exploit the farmer. So even if entrepreneurs have great solutions and offerings for farmers, generally it is an uphill task to first win their trust.

6. **So many schemes for financing on paper but very difficult to get access:** Either due to high demand or low supply, access to many of the schemes is difficult without having the right connections.

7. **Large or known farmers get most of the attention:** This could explain the coexistence of so many schemes and initiatives on the one hand and so many farmers being unaware of them on the other. This was brought up by many farmers across states I spoke to. That most of the extension work (extension officers or KVKs) is really limited to some large farmers or 'known' farmers, and the rest rarely get any attention or information.

8. **Land aggregation or CF hindered by diversity of crop and seed:** On paper, the benefits of scale are great. But CF is not easily workable, as all farmers don't grow the same crops and will not agree for this mingled approach. Even for mass procurement, scale is not achievable if there is no standardization of the seeds they all use for example. Lastly, for selling economies of scale, a large volume of the same crop is needed to be provided at one place. It is not possible if small farms of diverse crops are spread out over many villages (e.g., in some FPOs).

9. **Best practices sharing is key:** Even the very progressive farmers feel that the one thing they lack is getting exposure to best practices at other farms across the country. Even farmers who are taking full benefit of extension and KVK efforts feel that it would do them a whole lot of good if such trips were organized to take farmers across states to showcase highly successful farms where they could understand methods and learn from those farmers.

10. **CHCs and godowns can solve huge, small farmer problems:** Many progressive farmers who have organized themselves into FPOs/FPCs feel that the two most important things needed for every FPO to have are a CHC (with latest equipment) and small local warehouses to store their produce to avoid distress selling.

11. **Village governance question marks:** Over the years, the power centre in the villages has moved to the panchayat and the sarpanch from the NGOs in the past. However, many farmers say that the BDOs and the sarpanch are not devoting the time and attention to the farmer community as needed. A farmer in Gujarat told me that he felt that the gram panchayat sahayak spent 90 per cent of his time on non-farmer-related paperwork and hence had not time for the farmer. If the sarpanch and the panchayat are the most important last-mile link to the farmer, such feedback needs to be noted.

12. **Shrinking holdings leads to exit from farming (even for big farmers):** What is thought is a 'small farmer' issue turns out to have relevance for large farmers too. The fact that with passage of time, land parcels keep shrinking as they get divided between family members and family size keeps growing, if the income per acre of land is not growing, it is not enough for a growing family and forces the family to diversify income stream and look for other avenues. Even a farmer owning 50 acres of land felt that it was inevitable and that was a big deal I thought.

13. **The low take-up of current crop insurance is an opportunity:** One of the largest farmers I spoke to paid about ₹50,000 per year as crop insurance premium but to cover only 20 per cent of his land. He has been reducing his coverage over the years, as he sees no benefit of it at all. He feels that the mechanism the insurance companies use to accept a claim (loss must be experienced by all the villages in an area, not just one village or farm) is flawed

and rarely results in an approved claim. I have heard this view often. Such farmers are willing to pay the premiums. Hence, this is an opportunity for new fintech companies who can offer insurance and pay out claims based on technology.

14. **It takes only a little nudge to come back:** A very eye-opening experience was when I met two sets of people over a gap of few months. One set returned to family farming in 2019 after staying jobless for some time despite college degrees. Another set of farmers was forced to return to their farms during the lockdown in 2020. Both these sets of people had re-embraced farming with a lot of passion. I realized that just a nudge is needed to get some of the farmers back. Positive propaganda, hence, can have this very positive effect.

15. **Horticulturists more progressive?** This is food for thought, I feel. On balance, I have seen horticulture farmers to be much more positive about their farms and growth than those growing food grains or pulses. I believe that it is because of the inherently higher profitability of such crops and the fact that such farmers are already doing well without much government support.

16. **Lot of value to be added in intercropping guidance:** One area which appears to have been missed out by current extension channels is that of deeper training and skill transfer on increasing number of crops. Even very progressive farmers have pointed this out as one of the very few things they feel they need more help on. This is evident in my assessment of the landscape too. It is a white space, I feel.

17. **Assurance of price and quantity in advance:** *Mandi* is the buyer of last resort. Many farmers have said that they are open to engaging with direct buyers but have not heard from them. Just some premium over *mandi* prices will not be enough for them, unless the buyer can assure

offtake of certain quantity regularly. If it is conditional buying and someday their crop arrival is not up to the mark, they will still have to run to the *mandi* with it. Such unpredictable arrangements will not help farmers. This is where contract farming could be the better solution.

18. **Water is usually the main constraint in taking multiple crops:** A sustainable way to increase income is to take more than one crop. But most times, the constraint is not knowledge or ability or skill, but it is the lack of water. If it is a rainfed area, at best a second crop can be taken.

19. **Local state government can make a big difference:** A farmer's fortunes not only depend on Central government policies but can also be affected a lot by what the state government does or does not do. I have seen stark differences in policies or push made by different states, and it has resulted in starkly different outcomes for the farmers. On comparing two states of very similar agroclimatic conditions, one has put farming as a thrust area (Himachal Pradesh) giving farmers a lot of grants and incentives (to buy equipment), while the other (Uttarakhand) has not encouraged horticulture to that extent.

20. **Chakbandi:** Many states in India still have fragmented land parcels owned by farmers. This prevents them from carrying on efficient farming. *Chakbandi* refers to redistributing landholdings between farmers by the state government to make holdings contiguous. I heard at least two farmers (Uttarakhand and even Maharashtra) tell me about this problem. While many states have done it, it should be addressed by all soon.

21. **Advice and handholding:** One of the most consistent and widely mentioned points one hears from almost all the farmers is that they are open to trying a lot of new things,

however small their farm may be, but they need sound advice and someone to guide them and hold their hand. And they are willing to pay.

22. **'Everyone thinks differently':** Another blatant reality on the ground in villages is that even within a particular village, getting people together to work collectively is not very easy. They have not done it in the past and are habituated to doing their own thing. Strong leadership or case studies and success stories showcasing at national media level are required to convince them, otherwise to join hands. It's not so much problem of trust but that of inertia towards change. Some NGOs who have been working for decades at grassroots level across the country vehemently disagree and believe that farmers are willing to and want to work together; they just need leadership. These two opposing views are both coming from the ground—and are both true.

23. **Global piece is missing:** Current agritech education available to the farmer is only focused on domestic research and knowledge. There is very little focus on global trends and practices which can be shared with farmers. One very progressive farmer I met had been sent to Australia recently as part of a learning opportunity and realized how sugarcane is fully sown and harvested by machines, while in India most cane farmers don't make money as they do it all manually at a very high cost. Farmers are asking for global updated inputs on methods, mechanization and business models and want to emulate.

24. **Not all farmers want their kids to leave farming:** Even a 4-acre farm owner in Maharashtra feels that his son could make double the money in farming than what his son could make in a city job. Another 5-acre farm owner in Gujarat said that his daughter could make 5 times the

money on the family farm than in a job—and this is very encouraging from a grain drain or reverse grain drain perspective and confirms my view that often only a nudge may be all you need.

25. **New agritech start-ups have a long way to go:** Despite hundreds of start-ups, not many famers have heard of them. In fact, only a handful had been approached for using online marketplaces or by finance companies. Even people at KVKs have not received many proposals for them to try some technology which can then in turn be proposed to the farmer. It also means that most agritech start-ups have focused on a few states (Karnataka, Madhya Pradesh and Maharashtra) and need to widen their scope.

26. **Happy to pay for his time! (Profit-sharing arrangements are welcome):** Many farmers I met are very open to exploring flexible profit-sharing arrangements which can be made. Sharing 10–15 per cent of the benefit a farmer gets with a farm advisory or management company is not unthinkable for them.

27. **Power, fuel and DIY:** With increasing cost of diesel, the total cost of using machines such as tractors and tillers is going up. Most new devices used in agritech will need charging, and such access may be low. Solar or electric power on the farm is hence important. Keeping the apparatus and software simple and something farmer can 'control' and not feel intimidated by is also the key.

28. **Online courses are most welcome:** It is another strong feedback which has stood out across my meetings. Almost all farmers have felt that an ongoing, short-duration, easy-to-access practical course on agriculture techniques would be a hugely positive thing. They can access it online over their phones or laptops and would be happy to pay for it too, especially if their children start using it. It is another white space I see potential for, another white space.

29. **Need for high quality advisory services:** For advisory services, farmers are looking for actionable, timely, relevant, accurate and high-quality inputs, information and advices, which are accessible easily and round the clock. Tough customer? Well, effort is required to make an impact.

CURRENT STATE OF ADOPTION

Below is a short summary of the sense of the current state of adoption I get from all the on-ground interactions.

1. Most small-to-medium farmers are using tractors on their farm, either owned or hired.
2. Two-thirds to three-fourths farmers are dependent on the rains and take one or maximum two crops a year.
3. Some large farmers are using implements for sowing and harvesting as well.
4. Very few farmers are using advanced machinery for drying produce or treating the soil for multicropping.
5. Many medium-to-large farmers have proper storage and drying infrastructure or even threshing and sorting infrastructure on their farms to minimize PHLs.
6. Some medium-to-large farmers have handling, packing, sorting and grading machines in-house.
7. FPO membership, extension office engagement and KVK engagement is low.
8. Very few farmers are leasing in land to aggregate it.
9. Almost no one has fully embraced online buying and direct or online selling.
10. Precision farming awareness and use are very low.

BUT SOMETIMES THE FARMER IS MORE TECH-SAVVY THAN YOU THINK

The last few months I spent across several states in India and meeting farmers of all scales and sizes, the one thing I realized was that in general many of them are a lot more tec-savvy than we think. Whether it is the 16-year-old daughter of a farmer in Himachal, who promptly started googling some Israeli agritech start-up name I gave her, or the farmer in Madhya Pradesh, who joined a two-week course at a KVK with his son, or the extremely small farmer (less than 1 acre) in Uttarakhand, who is proactively meeting his block officer regularly and planting varieties of broccoli in his farm, on balance I have been pleasantly surprised on their awareness and hunger to learn more and try new things. Access to the Internet over smartphones and the presence of a young adult in the house who is involved are no doubt some of the key drivers of this, and it has provided a great springboard to move forward and upward from here. We should not waste this positive mindset that farmers are in.

CHAPTER 11

UNDERSTANDING THE FARMER'S PAIN POINTS AND LOOKING FOR THE SWEET SPOT

Ground-up Story: Pain Points, Sweet Spots and Water in the Cotton!

Yadav Singh is on the board of one of the FPOs in Madhya Pradesh. It had about 2,000 farmers and 10,000 acres under its fold. He has his own farm of about 40 acres and leases in another 20 acres for ₹10,000 per acre per year. The agreement is on a written basis with a stamp on it but not registered anywhere. He says that in villages, people trust each other and don't need agreements. But he said that they had devised a mechanism by which the landlord would feel secure. He gave him a large amount as a deposit upfront for three years which would generate him the annual rent out of interest and acted as a security (the deposit would be about 20%–25% of the value of the land). After the three-year lease period was over, he would take the deposit back. I thought that it was a smart and fair way of creating mutual comfort. My conversation with Yadavji was a broad-based one, trying to touch upon a lot of areas as I wrapped up my research for the book. And the idea was to get as much insight from him and just listen to his point of view. 'We have an acute shortage of combined harvesters and even onion sowing machines available for rent which many farmers are very keen to hire and use.' He said that the onion machine was a must-have, as it saves them about ₹10,000 per acre as he would need 100 farm workers working for 2–3 days to just sow 1 acre with onion. Clearly, rent could be high for such an equipment. He said that just simple tractors nowadays cost about ₹1,000 per hour vs ₹600–₹700 a few years ago. Diesel prices are biting them. His concern with contract farming was one of quality and offtake. Few years back, the contracting customer refused to pick up the crop of maize because of some quality issues, and farmers had to fall back on the *mandi*. There must be a channel to sell subquality produce, as farmers would inevitably have such episodes which is not in their control. When I probed him a bit more about customers not honouring their commitments, he shared with me an odd incident where farmers were adding water to their own cotton crop to increase its weight—it was bound to happen that the customer would realize it and not accept it. He said that sometimes it's difficult to make all farmers fall in line with good practices. He also said something which I had by then heard innumerable times: 'Top-level planning is easy; it's this kind of ground-level challenges that are very difficult to deal with.' On a positive note, he felt that the youth in the villages was showing more interest but needed proper training and education on agriculture and new practices. They needed help for that. He said that the FPO was facilitating wholesale buying of their produce, and the farmer got fair price in a week with proper weighing of their produce, proper grading as well as lower transporting costs. 'We have just got sanctions for funds to build a warehouse under the FPO and we will be able to get even better prices for farmers. It is a very positive development, and we are looking forward to it.' He felt that farming had now become a business which required investment. If a farmer has one bad year, they are out of action for three, and that's when many of them are willing to lend out their land, as they can't afford to invest. My last question to him was about their interactions with the nearby KVK centre. He said that it was 40 km away, and most farmers didn't have the time or money to spend and visit it. If someone could come to their local collection centre and hold training workshops on cultivation related issues, it would be extremely useful. In fact, he asked me if I could come and organize a class every six months. He said that he would get at least a few hundred farmers to attend, and they would be happy to even pay for it! I asked him why he could not ask the KVK staff to come and do similar workshops as the head of the FPO. He said that he had not thought of that. He was buying pesticides from a friend in Maharashtra and saving about 50 per cent on the price. I assumed that it was for the FPO, but it was for his own farms. He said that he was then planning to share that with the FPO farmers too.

This really sums up a lot that I have tried to put together across the book: that there are several good things already available, but there are some gaps—we must focus on them and move ahead.

IN SEARCH OF THE SWEET SPOT

In the previous two chapters, we have summarized the characteristics of the farmers in general, their thought process around agritech and some key needs which they are looking to fill as well as areas which they are open to learn and adopt.

A list of the 'low-hanging fruit', where the farmer is keen to change and will find it easy to change, is being presented. We also draw out the specific pain points of the farmer (which in another sense are the needs which must be addressed but also the kind of constraints which they face in moving ahead). We put those two things together to provide a 'path' to crystallize what the solution set should look like. This part will pull out what they 'can do', while the above chapters focused on what they 'can't do'. I call it the sweet spot. Maximum thrust of entrepreneurs, government as well as students entering the field should be on this area. Areas which may not really be suitable to the Indian situation and would be futile to pursue by various stakeholders have been mentioned too.

When looking at the sweet spot for agritech in India, it is best to make a matrix on two parameters. One is the kind of farmer, which is mainly to do not only with the size but also other things. And the second is the position of the product or service on the value chain. If we plot all our inputs based on this matrix, we get a very interesting 'target map' which can be very useful to policymakers, entrepreneurs and, even more importantly, to students of agribusiness and technology. This is not a science though, so even if we get a good sense of the 'clusters' which are ripe and low-hanging fruit ready for the picking, it will be an important milestone in this journey.

SEGMENTING IS IMPORTANT

For this purpose, I have segmented the farmer into four buckets: small (less than 1 hectare), medium (1–5 hectare), large (5–50 hectare) and very large (>50 hectare). While I have classified the value chain in certain ways in the previous chapters (5 and 6), for this purpose, I have used the following eight subsegments: mechanization, hired equipment, input purchase, smart farming, advisory and information sharing, fintech, storage and market access. Table 11.1 summarizes the sweet spots based on intensity of need of the farmer.

Farmer	Mechanization	FaaS	Inputs	Smart farming	Advisory and information	Fintech	Storage	Market access
Small	+	+++	+++	+	+++	+++	+++	+++
Medium	++	+++	+++	+	+++	+++	+++	+++
Large	++	++	++	++	+++	++	+++	+++
Very large	+++	+	++	+++	+++	++	+++	+++

Table 11.1. Farmer Agritech Adoption Dashboard

The key points emerging from this adoption dashboard are as follows:

1. **Areas like advisory and information services, storage solutions and novel market access:** These are clearly needed by all segments of farmers, and there is a clear pull for that. These should be the first ones to be launched and made available by the various stakeholders. Given that the need intensity and receptivity are high, service providers will be able to charge a fair price for it too. Advisory and information services is a very broad area, covering not only basic price, weather and acreage info for small farmers but also best practices, new case studies and success stories from elsewhere in India and overseas. Similarly, advisory can straddle across the spectrum of procurement, cultivation and marketing and should have the capability to go very deep into technical matters and technology, so that it can maximize its customer base—and cross-subsidize pricing for some who can afford to pay lesser. Online educational courses are a sweet spot too.

2. **Input access services, renting of equipment (FaaS) and financial services:** These are the three segments with very high appeal as well. Most FPOs who are even just aggregating demand for about 1,000 small farmers can get about 10 per cent reduction in input costs. Aggregators and marketplaces must enable a smooth process (delivery as close to the farm as possible) and try to beat the 10 per cent improvement in price they already get. Input purchase is closely linked to financing. Also, well-priced and effective insurance policies, where village-specific and farm-specific damage are also covered, will have a lot of takers. Finally, FaaS is in huge demand by the FPOs for the small farmers particularly, but interest is across the board. Clearly, the smaller the farmer, more sensible

for them to rent. The government CHC initiative is the right one, and financing of it must be worked out. So this package of all inputs (including rented equipment) and its financing is definitely a sweet spot.

3. **Mechanization and smart farming:** This feature is low on the list because it is less viable for the small farmer directly, buying outright large new equipment or getting into smart farming with the use of data, AI, IoT, sensors, drones, etc. But the demand, interest and affordability by the large and very large farmers for both these services are high. Given the large numbers, even this segment is close to 1 million farmers (0.56% own more than 10 hectares). Even the small farmers want this but will become a viable target market once they are able to come via the 10,000 (soon to be 20,000) FPO/FPCs as that business model settles down and each FPO is able to have a CHC. Demand for high-end automation and farm mechanization equipment and the market for it in India can be quite large. Harvesting, planting, sowing, transplanting, weed removing machines and robots involved in this can find quite a good customer base. These companies may have to take the approach via agriculture research institutes and KVKs, as well as a bottom-up education to create the pull. Even 50–100-acre farmers are very highly mechanized with just 4 people running a 100-acre farm. This is not uncommon. Precision agriculture for small farmers is the key. I want to highlight 'soil testing and analysis' as a small but key part of the 'smart farming' approach—in fact, the very starting point, even before a farmer can decide on their inputs. A very large number of farmers all over India have not got their soils tested at all or not done it recently. Either they are not aware or the government facility is overburdened and unable to get to them. Hence, there is robust demand for a private enterprise to serve this market and link it to other post-testing advisory services on crop and nutrient selection.

There are companies who have launched such services, and there is room for many more. Deeper solutions for intercropping and multicropping are white spaces too. Finally, I would say that as a customer segment itself, the rural youth is in itself a very big, sweet spot and hence should be focused on, given that they are more tech-savvy as well.

SOME GENERAL CONCLUSIONS AND POINTERS

It is also important to note here that of the four segments, even the smallest farmers are ready customers—even without the need for FPOs or finance. They have the willingness to pay, and the value proposition offered to them will create the ability to pay. This is quite a big insight. Most of the current wisdom and assumption on this is that this segment is tough to do commercial business with. To be sure, small farmers are of a few types: (a) those who have low focus on the business, as I classified in Chapter 10, can be carved out while preparing go-to market strategies and (b) there are others who are focusing on agriculture but are unaware or have not given serious thought to it and those who feel that it may not benefit them as much. These are the fence sitters—relatively low-hanging fruit and a little effort will reap big success.

Another important part is that even for the more risk-averse agribusiness companies, who will not venture into small farmers, the large-to-very-large farmers are a very viable target audience. Hence, businesses should not focus on B2B business models only. Large farmers are more than ready to adopt their offerings.

OUT OF BOUNDS AND WHY

On the flip side, there are some pockets on the farmer/segment continuum, where either the demand is very low or adoption is going to be a very slow process.

1. **Highly rainfed areas with only one-crop potential:** There are several agri-zones in India which have very low irrigation penetration and are mainly rainfed. Such farmers face acute shortage of water. And rainwater harvesting or building canals is too expensive a solution. Hence, they find it very difficult or almost impossible to take more than one crop in a year.[1] Globally, only 5 per cent of rainfed arable land has multicropping, while 40 per cent of irrigated land is able to do it. They will not be able to use much of the advisory, FaaS or other services that most other small farmers would be able to.

2. **Choose your state:** As mentioned before, it's not all about Central government policies and push to farming. The state governments play a very critical, in fact a make or break, role. If a particular state government administration is not very focused on this area and its incentives and efforts are low compared to other states, it is better to position yourself in a state where the tailwind is positive. Because even if the farmer is willing to make changes, other issues will render them less competitive.

3. **Choose the correct route—avoid bottoms up:** Sometimes, it is best to avoid the farmer first, and start from the top. Companies particularly focused on the machinery and smart farming segment and need to deploy hardware and devices on the farms may need to approach the government to facilitate testing and trials at the Central or state level, so the word about the new technology can be easily spread across the state or country faster.

4. **Avoid complex solutions:** Stakeholders, even those focusing on large farmer segment, should avoid devices which are difficult to use, connect (telecom) and power (battery or solar operated). Even the CTA report has

---

[1] https://en.wikipedia.org/wiki/Multiple_cropping

said that one should provide one or two simple pieces of information which address the core problem, rather than overwhelm the farmer with too much data and information. Another aspect to this is that solutions being offered, internationally or even homegrown ones, have certain data as a prerequisite but a lot of such data may not be available to start with and not even in the medium term. A classic example is farm-level title data or history of farm output patterns. Even advisory services may need access to certain information which may not be available. Years of hard work is needed to launch such solutions. Some start-ups are already investing time and money on it (e.g., CropIn). But this space may not get us the early wins we are looking for.

5. **Don't reinvent the wheel:** Many medium-to-large farmers are using some mechanization and modern methods. It would be a mistake to go in with your solution with no regard to what they are already doing. It is best to try to solve their problem in the existing situation, rather than suggest starting something from scratch. Hence, listening to them and building from what they have will see more take-up and receptivity. Second, almost all farmers also feel that they know their subject matter the best. Use their knowledge to plug it into your solution. The CTA report has again opined that one should involve the existing extension staff. Also promote continuation of traditional information-gathering or knowledge-sharing practices.

This sums up the various sweet spots to focus on and the longer-term spaces which should be avoided initially and taken up in the next phase. The next chapter attempts to provide a pathway to bridging the gaps.

PART VI

CLOSING THE LOOP WITH ALL STAKEHOLDERS TOGETHER

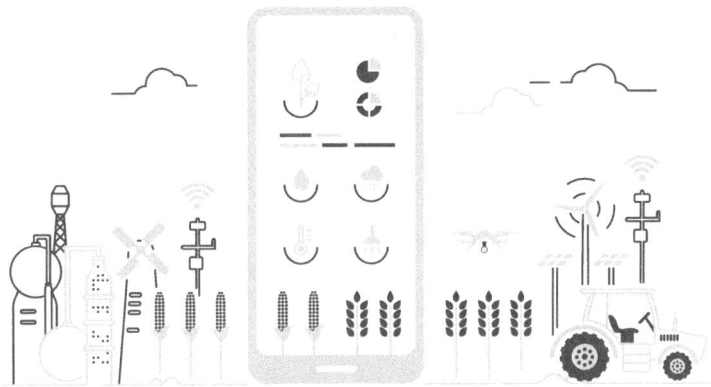

CHAPTER 12

BRIDGING THE GAPS AND PROVIDING A PATHWAY

Ground-up Story: 'I Don't Like Farmers Who Offer Me Tea'

Mr Lal is a senior agriculture professional who has worked for 30 years in Bihar at the grassroots level and has seen farming and its challenges very closely. But he is a very progressive person, and our hour-long conversation was really full of insights. He had given me a specific time to call, but when I could not get through, he called right back, profusely apologizing for the delay. We exchanged courtesies and settled down into the discussion. I asked him to start right at the beginning with the soil. He told me how the Soil Health Card (SHC) programme had a lot of promise, as it was supposed to be auto scanned at the input dealers shop and automatically it would instruct the dealer what to dispense to the farmer. But only 15–20 per cent of the farmers in his area had got SHCs done. He blamed both supply constraints and non-cooperation by farmers. He also said that sample collection must be done by trained professionals, as often samples were not taken well, resulting in two farms with similar output showing different soil results. Farmers' trust in the SHC also dropped. *Kisaan salahkaars* (farmer advisors) were appointed for every block, and a lot of information exchange was happening, but that has now reduced, as bulk of the time, these advisors are busy in other work at the block office. He said that there was a need for more trained advisors to go to the villages and spend time with them on such things. I asked him about advice on cropping patterns and selection. He said that the focus must be on training farmers on *risk management,* so whichever crop they choose, they can manage the outcomes. This really resonated with me. Our discussion then moved to the KVKs and how much they were engaged with farmers on new technology education. I was surprised to hear how some crops take two–three years before they can be grown by the farmer after the testing is done by KVKs on their model farms. I asked him how he finds the right-minded farmer to pursue these progressive activities with. He said, 'I don't like the farmers who invite me home for tea! They have all the time in the world and only want to know how they can benefit from schemes. I like the farmer who makes me wait hours while he is busy on the farm. It is such farmers who may vent out their frustrations but once they listen to our ideas and get it … they actually are the one who will try out new things and even if things go wrong, don't blame anyone, but try to improve further!'

This conversation is so apt, and it leads me to this chapter on bridging the gaps between the demand and supply of agritech offerings and thinking of the pathways which will help us to do that.

NOW HOW TO GO ABOUT IT?

The best way out is possible only if both the user (farmer) and the supplier (entrepreneur/government) understand what is needed and meet on common ground. The differences existing between the demand (what the farmer is able and willing to adopt) and the supply (what is being offered by agritech companies or government) will be enumerated to bring out the gaps which are needed to be filled. Università Bocconi in Italy has summed up the approach quite well: 'Understanding the intended users, ensuring economic viability, fully promoting the service and making sure the technology offered is the right solution to the problem.'

A COMMON GROUND THAT EXISTS TO GENERATE EARLY ADOPTION

In any initiative which is complex and long drawn, it is crucial to keep all the stakeholders engaged and motivated. These stakeholders include all the government departments which are implementing various schemes for promoting new methods to improve farmer economics. It also includes all the NGOs which are doing grassroots work with the farmer as well as all the new agritech entrepreneurs in India who have set up shop to address this opportunity and also those global companies which are looking to enter with their cutting-edge solutions. There is no question that the road is long drawn and there will be ups and downs of implementation and setbacks. Hence, need for keeping the motivation high is very crucial. For government agencies, this may mean getting the chance to keep the funding going for their schemes. Likewise, for agripreneurs (agriculture + entrepreneur = agripreneur), their sponsors will need to see early successes as well to keep funding further rounds of growth. And most importantly, early successes will keep the farmer engaged and motivated to spread the word around. This can only happen with going for 'early successes' and 'celebrating' them. Both are equally important. Failures and setbacks must be internalized, and successes and promising milestones have to be celebrated and broadcasted far and wide. Often, we do the opposite.

Early success stories come from the early adopters. Early adoption will come if we all focus on the easy wins (fast achievement of high impact). Given that we are talking about agriculture here, it is inherently a long gestation period activity. But even within that, the operator will have to be smart and pick the ones which are not only in the sweet spot but can also show faster results. Nothing succeeds like success is a proverb which probably works even better in the rural and agrarian setting where scepticism is high, and trust is low. Seeing is even more important for believing. Which basically means that we must create poster children and champions who become brand ambassadors and act like magnets to attract more farmers to be optimistic and to experiment.

Here, I outline some of those opportunities and areas which we should focus on first.

1. Choose the mid-sized farmer as initial target market, as they are aspirational for most small farmers and not someone they cannot relate to. This has resonated with many ground-level experts too. Highlighting the success story of a large farmer is of no use, as farmers will attribute the success to their wealth and size of farm and not the technology under review. In fact, there is a programme under the KVKs called the 'exposure visits', where best practices and success stories are showcased by taking farmers to the model farm. For this, the KVK makes it a point to choose only small farmer successes, and they agree to this point that such knowledge sharing results in explosive replication and emulation.

2. Choose farms in many diverse states, so maximum farmers can identify with it, and it is not seen as something which is not mainstream but a fluke or due to some very local characteristics.

3. Choose a solution which involves a larger group of farmers if possible—FPOs, leasing arrangements and collectives. This is a weak link in the villages, and stories of success from group activity will boost the image of such and bring positivity around it.

4. Choose an area where the benefit is very tangible and can be traced back to the new approach unequivocally.
5. Choose an area where farmer involvement is there and it is easy to implement, so that they feel that it is something they can do more of.
6. Once these 'champions' achieve the results, state and Central governments should launch very-high-octane propaganda to make sure all district-level farmer leaders and panchayat officials know about it and discuss these success stories.
7. The private sector should be equally involved in this propaganda, as their interest is fully aligned with the farmers. More farmers join in, the more opportunity there is.

With these broad thoughts, I have listed down some of the differences which exist, before I go on and suggest a step-by-step pathway.

Where Are the Differences

In Chapter 8, I highlighted five areas where the Indian agritech companies have not focused much on vs their global peers. Here, I am highlighting some areas where small and large farmers have an immediate need, but companies or schemes are not yet covering those fully. Figure 12.1 highlights the gaps to be bridged.

From the 'Farmer Agritech Adoption Dashboard' table in Chapter 11, I propose that agencies (private, government and NGOs) focus on just four areas first.

1. Mechanization

    (a) *Renting of equipment/FaaS business model:* This change can bring about quick results, which can be seen very soon within few months of a sowing or harvesting cycle itself. Drop-in requirement of

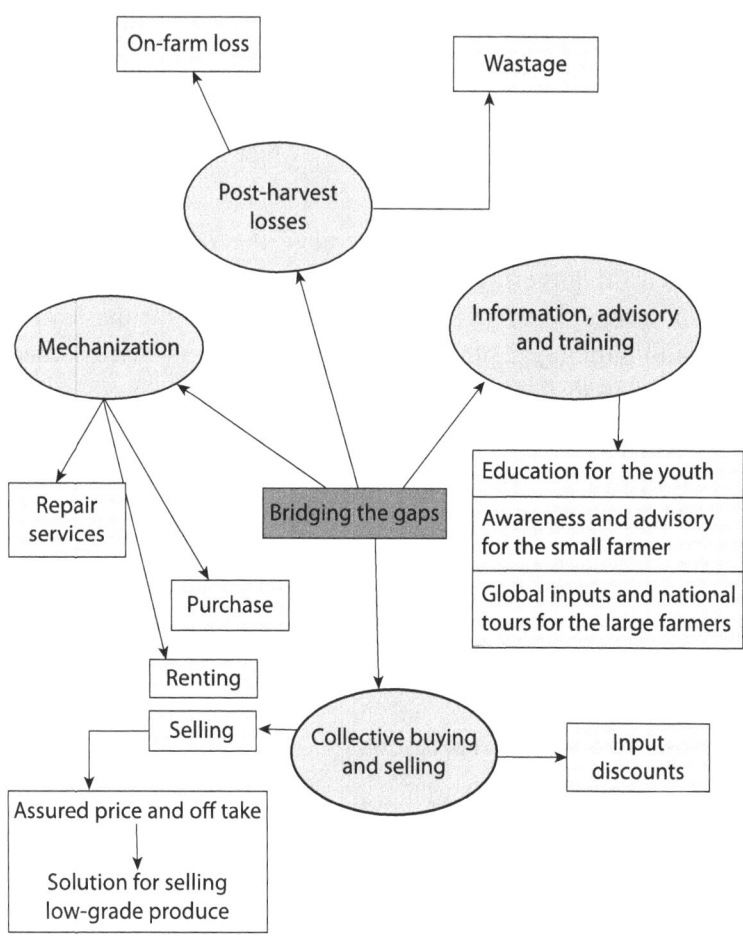

Figure 12.1. Bridging the Gaps between Supply and Demand

labour or ability to plant or cover more acreage due to machine availability will give positive impact very soon. The government has the CHC scheme, which NGOs and FPOs are trying to implement at grassroots levels. But agripreneurs who are in this field should accelerate the reach and marketing of this service. The Tractor Manufacturers Association (TMA) should also take the lead in this to tie up with private and public entities to make available the entire gamut of equipment and tools at a reasonable price and rental, maybe using entry pricing approach. Often FPOs and NGOs have told me that they don't have money, and the government should give them grant to buy equipment at the FPO level. I do not think that it is necessary. The FPO has the power to aggregate demand of thousands of farmers, and they should use this to negotiate and give assured visibility of offtake to original equipment manufacturers (OEMs) or other FaaS companies, who will find this invaluable. If the FPO/NGO can estimate that demand of which tool is needed in what quantities just by 1 cluster of 1,000 farmers, that will be a boon to the supply side. The OEMs and FaaS companies should then work closely with FPOs/NGOs to make available the equipment. As I have suggested, targeting a few mid-sized farmers under every KVK (about 700 of them) is enough, as long as the success story is being shared loudly and widely.

(b) *Machinery repair and maintenance:* An extremely crucial but totally ignored point, which is the key stumbling block to increased adoption of mechanization, is the total lack of after-sales services for the machinery. Most of the new machinery used today is from Punjab, as the old indigenous machinery industry which was bullock attached is no longer in use. Selling agents for this new machinery are located everywhere, but for even the smallest problem post sales, the technician has to come down from Punjab. It may take weeks for them to arrive, and the farmer cannot wait that long during their sowing or harvesting season. So they often revert to their old ways. Most times, farmers buy equipment under government grants, where up to 90 per cent is sometimes available. But once, after a year, if the machine has a problem, 100 per cent of the repair cost must be borne. That really pinches. And this again drives them back to their old ways.

2. **Collective buying and selling:** This is the other easy-to-achieve change which can show immediate, quantifiable results for farmers, small and large, and create pull for more change. Smart negotiation with input companies (seed, fertilizer and pesticide) is required to deliver tangible discounts. Scale achieved by FPOs or private sector aggregators can lead to much larger discount of 10–15 per cent and create a positive spiral of change. A stronger way of improving realizations is, of course, to help the farmer sell some value-added produce. A senior grassroots worker once mentioned the tag line he used to motivate farmers—*Dhaan nahin chawal bechenge,* meaning we will sell dehusked and without-bran rice, not the raw paddy. Such small interventions (putting up a milling machine to remove the husk and bran) can show farmers immediate benefits. The improvement in realizations can be very high in such a case. Overall, market access is probably more difficult to achieve than production-enhancement solutions. Hence, even production-focused solutions should focus on helping the farmer produce differentiated products which are easy to sell (organic or traceable).

3. **Advisory and information services:** This, I think, should be a bigger thrust area in the first stage itself. While there are many companies in this space, it should get more attention. The way to do this is to approach the two extremes first and fill the middle layer later. Within this, I believe that one gap is the focus on 'education' for the youth. Overall extension advisory, which is a more longer duration process and will show only gradual results, could be done later. Online training apps which can be accessed on phones and teach basic and intermediary skills to the youth and adults from a vocational perspective could

have a very high 'feel-good' and 'trust-building' impact, even if the commercial impact is low on the farmer. For the service provider, this can be a paid service, as I have noted in my discussions that there is willingness to spend money, particularly if it involves their children. This could easily reach a very large base of farmer households, and hence even a small fee could be meaningful for vendors. With the support of SFAC or NABARD, agribusiness companies could also partner with extension officers, KVKs and ACABC centres to offer such training.

At the same time, there is an opportunity to create a quick impact by addressing the other extreme. High-end information and advisory services should be launched for the large farmers (up to 50 hectares) who are already progressive and very hungry for more. The service to them should focus on two main things: (a) global experience and inputs and (b) case studies and farm visits to leading farms in India.

The former can be done in the form of paid access to online subscription and the latter via roadshows where 10–20 large farmers from 10–15 key agri states at a time (about 150 farmers in 1 tour) can be taken to 3–4 such 'model farms' in batches. In fact, there could be a 'selection' process to make it competitive too. This will have a huge and multifarious impact. First, the farmer who is hosting other farmers will feel extremely recognized and motivated. Second, the farmers visiting the farms will get immediate learning by seeing things on the ground. Third, once these farmers get back to their villages, there will be a rub-off effect and word-of-mouth effect on the rest of them. The buzz that this 'event' will create in the village will lead to many more farmers wanting to be 'next'. These will prove commercial for the agripreneurs too, as they can charge for the global content and for hosting such 'best practices' trips. Why I stress upon some of these 'softer' initiatives is because one of the most powerful tools to make farmers adopt new technologies is 'word of mouth' and emulating neighbouring farmers. The word travels fast when someone is doing well in their community, and they all want to replicate it.

4. **Post-harvest loss-reduction technologies—under-focused, big impact[1]:** This is a very important area which has not received adequate focus yet. And it is a global phenomenon affecting high-income countries too. It is estimated that about 30–40 per cent of food produced globally is wasted. There are two contributors to this: loss in post-harvest and wastage at consumption points. While high-income countries experience more of the latter, India and other lower-middle income countries suffer more from the former, that is, loss of crop post harvest. The good news, though, is that this is easier to prevent than wastage is, because it happens on the farm and not spreads across the consumption centres. Key technologies used include timely harvesting, mechanized harvesting, threshing, handling, drying, storage and milling and even extend to transportation (cold chain, etc.). In fact, drying, storage and milling are where automation is giving maximum benefits to farmers.

But it was to my surprise that in a conversation with a KVK head, I was told that not much thought had gone towards this space in India. But he agreed that if such equipment could be made available on rentals, it could help the farmer reduce loss as well as get better prices for their sorted/graded product. The complex part is that some of these machines differ between crops. Again, solutions for perishables vs non-perishables are different. Some may require more on-the-farm solutions vs from-the-farm ones. Another weak link is the *mandis*, which

---

[1] Course on 'Global Postharvest Loss Prevention' by the University of Illinois Urbana-Champaign, offered on Coursera.

usually don't have cold storage infrastructure and lead to wastage. As all produce (fresh fruits and vegetables) does not get sold on arrival, loss due to rotting could easily be as high as 30–40 per cent. This needs to be improved with urgency, as the price a farmer gets depends on the wastage happening at the *mandis* too.

PROVIDING A PATHWAY FOR ITS ADOPTION

There are many solutions available which are appropriate and address a crucial need of the farmer. But even these have to be adopted step by step. In many cases, financial constraints will prevent a farmer from using many of the desired solutions or result in inability to even do a trial (small farms, long harvesting period, etc.). I have already discussed above which kinds of solutions and technologies are easier to adopt and can have a high impact. Hence, having a pathway to ensure this early adoption is important.

I will now dwell on a few routes by which adoption can be accelerated.

1. **Self-designed:** For the past many decades, the farmer community has been overwhelmed with multiple schemes and programmes by the government agencies, NGOs or private companies. Many of them do not feel that they have benefited because they continue to live in hardship and a subsistence living. Hence, when again a host of agencies and now even new breed agripreneurs approach them again with even the low-hanging, appealing and high-impact proposals, scepticism may still be high. My interactions have made me realize that the farmer must feel a sense of 'ownership' and that they have designed a proposal themselves. This 'buy-in' can have a very positive outcome in accelerating adoption. And I don't mean giving the farmer a 'sense' of ownership. But actually, before launching or making a proposal, home visits or

melas could be held. Grassroots competitions could be run to throw up ideas from within the community, and a consultative approach can pay high dividends.

2. **Linking price to benefits:** I am a strong believer in the fact that a long-term impact can be achieved only if the service provider is making reasonable profits. But it may mean sacrificing some short-term gains, which brings me to the topic of pricing for these new services. The best model is to 'align' your gains with those of the farmer. Let them know that you gain only if they gain. This can be achieved in various ways, and I won't go into details here. But a high-variable component in pricing and linking it to performance or benefits which are tangible and quantifiable is a tried and tested way. After-sales support is very precious to farmers and often discourages them from trying new services or equipment. Assurances of this must be given with evidence.

3. **Trials are a must:** Although I have said in an earlier section that precision farming should probably not be the first thing to address, even for the companies who are offering this, the sales cycle could be quicker if trials are done on the field and clear results are shown. This will convince them of the technology benefits.

4. **Hyper-localization:** Agricultural produce is a very heterogenous market. So selling to farmers is not easy. There are 28 states in India and 15 agroclimatic zones across the country. Even within that, farmers grow fruits, vegetables, grains, pulses, oilseeds and commercial crops. So there is a lot of diversity. Not only is local language localization required, but product and services which can suite their local weather, soil, cropping patterns and farming infrastructure (storage, transportation and market access) and available resources are also important. This poses a challenge to marketeers because, for scaling up, they are always looking out for standardized products

or services. But if vendors take a cluster approach, map out the 'similar' zones and then approach the market, one can still draw up a list of an adequately large addressable market to approach with maybe small variations in their offering.

5. **Customization:** Furthermore, some may have the tendency (farmers too) of directly trying out some international technologies. While I myself am a strong advocate of studying these, being aware and using them, customizing these technologies will be crucial. The various research institutions in India also focus on this, but more time could be spent on picking good technologies and adapting them to local conditions and then offering them to the farmers. This will also ensure less hiccups and faster acceptance and usefulness too.

6. **Dealing with the decision-maker:** Another path to faster adoption is talking to the decision-maker in the farmer's household. Usually, a farmer will not decide to do something new without consulting their fellow farmers and even the panchayat, sarpanch, other extension officers, BDO or even KVKs. It is very important that all these 'stakeholders' are involved or are part of the 'buy-in' during the outreach. But once this is done and the farmer is mulling over the proposal, they will be influenced by their family—parents, wife and children. My years of travel deep into rural India have shown me how important family members are to any major decisions, particularly those pertaining to income and spending. Hence, the government, NGOs and agripreneurs should all include the youth and the women folk in their education and outreach programmes. Involving the youth via their schools or holding awareness campaigns just focused on them or even involving AUs to share the knowledge and information about new solutions will help accelerate this process of adoption.

7. **Not a social service!** I don't mean this in jest. It has been seen in many lower-middle income countries such as Latin America and Africa that many well-intentioned, well-funded programmes run by very smart people met with a lot of early success but did not last, only because they did not have a model where they could be profitable themselves in a sustainable way. When the funding dried up, they had to wind up and shut a successful venture, leaving behind even more disappointed farmers. That is the last thing we want. Hence, business models being pursued by agripreneurs or even FPOs and NGOs should beware that if it cannot generate profits or be self-sufficient in a few years, it will be a futile exercise. They should not look at it as a social service. If this means that companies have to take a B2B route to make it sustainable, so be it.

If this approach is taken and pathways are followed by all the stakeholders, we will see a rapid change in the landscape.

CHAPTER 13

A MARRIAGE MADE ON EARTH

Ground-up Story: Bihar or Jharkhand?

Mr Sushil Pandey picked up my phone, and when I gave him the reference and the context, he was more than happy to talk. It was about 1 PM, but he did not seem in a rush to break for lunch. He told me that he was the CEO of an FPO in Bihar in 2014. SFAC was running the initiative and recruiting and training CEOs and board members. He was part of that cohort. He put together a 1,000-farmer FPO across 14 villages. The project was for two years, and the SFAC had provided funding for that period. I sat up in my chair and prepared for a long conversation of what all he had been doing at the FPO and understand the success and failures. So I began asking more detailed questions. He said, 'I don't have any idea!'

I was taken aback. 'How come?' I asked. And he then told me that he was then working for an NGO in Jharkhand! 'What? Sorry. Are you based in Bihar or Jharkhand?' He said that he had quit the FPO in 2016 and moved to Jharkhand.

As he recounted his story, he told me that the legal set-up, registration of the FPC, appointment of the board members and finally bringing together the farmers, all this itself took close to a year. By the time he started various initiatives, most of the funds were used up and the second year was coming to an end, and he was asked to leave and take up another assignment. In the short one-year period, he got the FPO a fertilizer dealership which reduced their cost from ₹310 a bag to ₹270—about 12–13 per cent reduction, which is not bad. Even for pesticides he got them a ₹7,000 subsidy under a particular scheme which was running. And before he could do other things, the funding dried up. All he needed was two more years, and a lot of his plans on marketing, better cultivation techniques, using more mechanization, etc., could have come to fruition. To build market linkages, a lot of market analysis is needed. Even for making collection points, you need staff. To participate in bidding, you need infrastructure. All this takes time and needs working capital support. I asked him why he did not stay back. Each farmer just had to pay ₹25 per month for him to get his salary. He did tell the board that he could not stay, as there was insecurity and uncertainty for him, and no one stopped him either. Now he is focusing on water conservation issues in Jharkhand to ensure water supply by raising ground water levels, so that farmers can take a second crop, but he still rues the fact that he could not complete what he started in Bihar, where the average farmer in his FPO owned about 1.5 acres of land. But what hits him more is the 'emotional damage' it inflicted on the farmers who were shown dreams of a better tomorrow and were left high and dry. 'Now they will not trust new ideas and promises,' he concluded. Some key asks he had were to help farmers learn to grow their own seed or teach them proper usage of the hybrid seed they were buying. Second was to help them with soil testing and work towards them taking a second crop as this would stem the migration to cities. And last was to develop allied agri-activities like dairy to have other sources of income in a bad year.

It seems like the marriage of government and farmers is not made in heaven; hence, it must be strived for here on the ground.

We have seen by now how important it is to find common ground between what technologies, solutions and institutional systems are available overseas, what local companies or government agencies have launched in India and finally what the farmer needs and is able to adopt fast. It is also clear that the smart way to accelerate this at a large scale is to get early successes and showcase them broadly. To do this, we must target farmers in a strategic way with elegant solutions which are practical to execute without much resistance by the farmer. This is of course hard work, much tougher than just launching globally successful solutions and praying that some will work. A more calibrated approach is needed which is time-consuming and difficult. I trust that the dos and don'ts, dashboard and sweet spots which I have outlined will go some way in helping with this and achieve desired outcomes. But we have to keep in mind that this is not a marriage made in heaven, but a union which has to be painstakingly built on the ground. Think of it as an arranged marriage rather than love at first sight!

SUPPLY WILL NOT CREATE ITS OWN DEMAND

The only way to succeed is always with your ears firmly on the ground and to keep adapting what works for each farming community. Also, there are so many different states in India growing different crops (grains, cash crops, horticulture, etc.), and they each have a different challenge and therefore a different 'sweet spot'. Scalability of a business, hence, will have to be understood and configured in a very different way, as there is no 'one size fits all'. This is not easy for any agripreneur to achieve, as even they have limited resources and are looking for a quick path to profitability, which makes them look for a quick and scalable solution. Often this leads them to also offer products and services which can have a global appeal and if that takes off, it has the risk that soon they will dilute their focus locally and pursue export opportunities.

This point also reiterates the importance of continuous propaganda, publicity and promotion. Local block officers and village key opinion leaders are best placed to locally highlight the benefits of embracing modern methods. There is no point talking about big bang stories which will overwhelm the farmer and sound like a pipe dream. It is best to share small incremental stories of nearby farms and villages where change has resulted into tangible benefits. The government at a state level as well as at the Central level also needs to run little broader campaigns around awareness building and, lastly, the agripreneurs should also invest time and money in holding open houses with the objective of sharing the solutions they have and what their brethren are doing in other villages or states.

Although, word of mouth is a very powerful channel; sometimes good news travels much slower than bad news. One senior NGO leader I was talking to was not aware of a very progressive farmer in his own state, who had mechanized all his operations and was leasing in large tracts of land and running a very efficient farming 'business'. I was surprised to note that even after some 500–1,000 agritech start-ups were operational in India (some people put that number at 3,000), not many of them were dealing with more than 5,000–10,000 farmers each. Hence, the spread is not linear. Once critical mass is achieved, and all the above broadcasting takes place, there could be a step function change in the penetration of these products and services.

LOCALIZATION IS KEY

Last but not least, localization is crucial. This point resonates across a few chapters. Just because some technology has worked well in Australia or Italy, it may not work well in India at all. It may sound counterproductive, but in some cases, one will have to reinvent the wheel and launch a solution from the ground up. This does not contradict the point I made in

Chapter 11, because in certain cases you cannot just import a successful technology if it is not suitable for a particular farming area in India. For example, a multicropping-enabling technology may not work in rainfed and non-irrigated areas, and you may have to look at a new way of doing it. Perhaps taking just one crop, but a higher value one (horticulture, organic or microgreens) may be the right solution.

Second, solutions will have to be customized but for a particular cluster. This could be just one village or could spread across states (so customized but also standardized). And businesses will have to launch maybe four or five kinds of offerings (including pricing plans and price points) to really cover a large footprint.

CLOSING THE LOOP AND BRINGING ALL STAKEHOLDERS TOGETHER

Clearly, there are multitude of stakeholders of this ecosystem: the farmer, Central government, state governments, agribusinesses, students, agripreneurs, FPOs and NGOs, research institutes and agencies, AUs as well as the financial services industry in general (lenders and insurers). Although all of them have the same objective—to increase the farmers' income—each one is often working in silos and on their own little focus area. In addition, many of these components do not necessarily trust each other due to lack of transparency or some history. Some of these stakeholders are just working towards achieving their targets (SFAC now rushing to achieve the 10,000 new FPO target) without looking at the ground reality. Some government initiatives want to empower the farmers and gram panchayats directly, while some NGOs feel that they are being left out of the programmes even as feedback providers.

Another issue which emerges from my research is that usually, the solution to all problems is seen as 'more financial support needed from the government'. Either the farmer needs or the FPO needs it. Even NGOs are in constant need for more funds. Start-ups need more money and so do the SAUs. The government (Central and state) can only do so much, and not more. Hence, just as we ask farmers to not depend on the government and build an independently sustainable business, even the other stakeholders should learn to do the same. NGOs/FPOs often think that they can succeed only if they get one more year of funds. They will always need that one more year. This is never going to end till they break away from this mentality.

The first step of any successful stakeholder involvement programme would be to consult all stakeholders before any decisions affecting them are being taken. For example, one of the criticisms against the three agri-reform bills of 2020 was that such consultation process was not followed. Indeed, to break the decades of scepticism that farmers have, a body in the Ministry of Agriculture with senior farmer representatives should be formed. And similar structures at the state level as well as in other rural policymaking teams should be formed. This will lead to more focused policy formation as well as save time in to-and-fro and post-announcement protests. Another way of doing it is to involve the farmer in the implementation of rural development projects directly. While this is happening to an extent via the NREGA projects as well as a lot of grassroots rural schemes done through the panchayat channel, some more thought could be given to this to increase the sense of ownership of the farmer in such things.

To bring all the stakeholders together, I suggest to take the following steps.

1. This sector must be given top priority, and the government has to go into a crisis mode (remember 1991 and the forex reserves problem). It is only then that implementation can accelerate.

2. Create a task force by taking representatives from all the key Central, state and research institutes, educational institutes and agencies. Include representatives from agribusiness and NGOs: farm workers, land renters and land aggregators, environment and social scientists, food companies, *mandis* and *adatiyas* (the middlemen and agents of the mandi). This should be an empowered group to not only make recommendations but also implement them.

3. Conduct a two-way field survey to impart information and seek feedback. If needed, use a large, private sector market survey and research companies who have the scale to do a nationwide survey.

4. Form a national team of block and panchayat heads who can between themselves share best practices of each state and their farmers as well as give feedback to the super task force and push down its message to their grassroots.

5. Bring back the 'Jai Kisan' campaign. As I mentioned in Chapter 12, it is crucial to hence bring back their faith in the system and the pride in farming. Just the way we still see campaigns saluting our defence service personnel, or to attract talent to it, we need more such campaigns glorifying and thanking our farmers too and making them and, more importantly, their children believe that farming is a crucial and noble profession and equally rewarding too. This will lift the spirits of the farmer, slowly build back trust and make them more open to working closely with the authorities again.

6. Focus on outcomes not on targets. Increasingly with big top-down push for agricultural reform and liberalization as well as modernization (all well intentioned), a collateral damage and unwanted consequence have been that many of the agencies start focusing on the targets, whether it is hybrid seed deployment or SHGs

or irrigation deployments or now even the case of the number of FPOs. While target-based planning is required in a large country like India, a little more focus on the outcome, that is, follow-up with farmers where all these things have been deployed or initiated, would be very beneficial. Monitoring the improvements and tracking farmer feedback on that are required.

I have kept this chapter short, as it touches upon many issues already discussed elsewhere in the book. It serves as a reiteration of some important points and a wrap-up of the insights received from various on-the-ground interactions over the last 11 years.

CHAPTER 14

HOW MODERN METHODS CAN CHANGE AGRICULTURE FOREVER

Ground-up Story: 20-time Yield per Acre and Other Stories

I was fortunate enough to have been introduced to this very interesting gentleman living in Chhattisgarh. A tissue culture scientist, he once approached some small tribal farmers who were making about ₹2,000–₹3,000 per year per acre from their farms. He told them that if they followed his advice, they could make ₹50,000! He was not expecting their reaction when they all turned and disappeared thinking some mad man had arrived. He realized his mistake and in the next meeting he told them that they could make ₹10,000. To this, the farmers reacted more positively and wanted to hear his ideas. Soon they followed his advice and started earning about ₹20,000 per acre per year. The key change he had suggested was not some high tech solution but just using better seeds and completely changing what they were growing—from rice to aromatic plants.

●

Another grassroots agriculture expert I spoke to who has been working all over the country in rural development projects echoed the same sentiment. He said that even as an FPO, other than focusing on input and output linkages, there is a lot of scope by just focusing on the farming itself and crop selection, multicropping and intercropping. The key is to choose the right crop based on market intelligence and differentiation. A 2—3-time impact can be created on the farmers' output and income. Organic produce with proper residual testing can also open many new doors.

•———————•

A young man in his 30s who belonged to a business family in Gujarat, after graduating, worked for 7–8 years in his family business (running a general store). But one fine day, he gave it all up and, with no prior background, bought a five-acre piece of land and jumped into organic farming. He built his house on the farm too, and now the whole extended family lives on the farm. He is practising several modern techniques, including not using fertilizers, rainwater harvesting as well as multicropping including grains, vegetables and fruits. He owns an electric scooter and is keen to use electric or battery-operated automation equipment on his farm. He regularly goes to the AU nearby and has done several short courses. He wishes that the local panchayat extension officer would have more time for the farmers like him who need more handholding. He is soon planning to buy the next-door farm too and build a permanent water pond to be able to take more crops. When I told him about the 45-day scheme run for vocational training of his children, he was all ears. He had not heard about it and requested me to send him all the details. He wanted his daughter, who studies food and nourishment junior college course at the same AU, to explore such vocational training. While farming is still not the main source of income for the whole family, he is confident that very soon that they will only focus on this and make enough income and savings.

No, this is not a sketch of an 'ideal dream farmer of 2050'; it is Kashyap Bhai from a village near Ahmedabad. He is real and his breed is growing!

I have chosen the above three stories with the intent to show how large the impact can be on a permanent basis of even very small interventions. Those modern methods can have a very sustainable positive impact.

I have taken you on a long journey in this book. At times it was straightforward and at times we had to go through a few hoops to reach the point of understanding we wanted to. The topic is vast, complex and evolving, with no perfect answers. It is time to draw our conclusions and wrap up this walk we took together. I have introduced the SOLID framework which forms the basis of our approach. It is not some magic wand, nor a foolproof, guaranteed or your money-back scheme, but a changed way of doing smart farming.

We started out to outline a SOLID framework for achieving the multiple challenges being faced by farmers in India. The action points and solutions finally boil down to a few simple things. First, 'choose your battles'; there are too many bodies doing too many things. We need to focus on two or three areas and go into a hyper-execution mode in them, picking your battles carefully. Second, go into overdrive to 'broadcast success stories' of small- to mid-sized farmers. And lastly, 'educate, train, advise and inform' the farmer with intensity and one point of accountability and implementation.

The way I see it is that if you have achieved the following understanding and insights, the effort on the book has been worthwhile. I have purposely reiterated time and again several of the key messages throughout the book, and it is not an editorial error. The idea has been to let the message sink in deeply into the reader's thoughts.

SUMMARY OF KEY CONCLUSIONS

- **The need for change:** A growing population needs a material increase in production, but resource availability is dropping and climatic conditions are changing, leading to a drop in yields. Environmental issues leading to increasing costs coupled with a reducing farmer population and farm sizes put constant pressure on the farmer's income. These are the imperatives forcing stern action. And use of modern farming systems is therefore crucial. And it is equally important to liberate the farmer by liberalizing farming activity in order to enable them to rise to the occasion.

- **How to think about 'modern farming':** I have classified modern farming to include agriculture technology, best practices used by farmers, new business models, mechanization as well as using new institutional frameworks such as eNAM, FPOs, contract farming and land lease. I have given a very wide definition on purpose, so that improvements can be achieved from any direction, including relooking incrementally at simple things such as crop selection and multicropping. At the same time, there are fallouts of adopting technology on the farms. It will need much lesser people, and hence the excess manpower will need to be redeployed gainfully and, second, the ability and affordability of agritech solutions will differ widely between farmer groups. This has the risk of increasing the rural digital divide and making the larger farmers even larger at the expense of the smaller farmers. This must be balanced, especially for a country like India.

- **Size does not matter:** Once farmers are open to learning about and adopting these new methods as well as updating themselves regularly, even a small and marginal farmer owning less than a hectare of land can lift up their income sustainably to have a decent and comfortable livelihood. Focusing on crop choice, lowering input costs, preventing on-farm losses, leasing in land for cultivation as well as joining hands with other farmers in collectives are the ways by which eventually the size will not matter and even the smallest of farmers can bring about a lot of improvement for themselves.

- **Sustainable change:** It is important to understand that we are in pursuit of a long-term sustainable solution, rather than tactical help for one or two bad years. It is possible to do this and reduce dependence on the government help as well as the vagaries of nature (irrigation, multicrop, allied services, greenhouse and hydroponics). After all, government help is ever-changing and never enough, if the farmer sticks to their current ways.

- **A SOLID farming model is possible:** It is just the way we approach it—with a medium- to long-term objective of providing a sustainable solution which helps to make farming activity lucrative and independent and causes a manifold increase in income.

- **Who will man the farms is the question:** World over, farmers are ageing, even as their children leave farming. This is equally true, if not more, even in India. Hence, the more important question to address is how to retain the interest of the rural youth to stick to farming and, in fact, embrace it with renewed vigour and training. Addressing key issues of profitability, awareness and training on modern systems is needed urgently. Everyone feels that the grass is greener on the other side. Dedication and pride for the family farm must come back. Attracting new farmers is another important way to achieve this. Once they decide to take up farming, they will have to do it very differently—using the 5 Ps framework—with pride, profits, pursue with independence, embrace the paradigm shift into modern systems, or play it differently with leasing in or leasing out their land. New farmers are already noticing the buzz in the industry and coming in, leaving their engineering or finance careers; it's a trickle now but has to be nurtured to grow bigger. The Italian experience is very pertinent here.

- **Assessing current landscape:** A thorough look at the global landscape of modern agriculture systems as well as experience of various countries in this pursuit throws up a lot of learnings. Comparing it with a nascent but prolific Indian landscape shows that almost all the key areas are being addressed and products and services are available. A review of the policy landscape overwhelms us when we learn how much has been done by the government across the spectrum and via a host of agencies and institutions over the last few decades. Reducing the number of agencies involved to sharpen the focus and increase accountability while keeping it simple to digest, for the farmer, is a must. An outcome-based approach vs a target-based one and a little increased focus on monitoring and feedback post implementation will go a long way. We can also learn from the number-oriented approach of China the need to build private involvement for scale—something the Latin American countries taught us—as well as the impact of overprotecting farmers from Europe. Participants will do well to pay heed to these experiences.

- **Ground-up stories:** The book has mainly focused on extensive ground-level meetings with farmers, FPOs, NGOs, government officials, academia and agribusiness companies. The focus though was on the inputs from the farmers themselves. The key insight is that the average farmer, on balance, is already using some or the other form of modern methods, but the overall awareness of the newer systems is very weak. At the same time, willingness and curiosity to try out new technology or even new business models is high. The need of education and handholding as well as ground-level leadership is what is required. But the process has to start from the farmer upwards. Even the newer FPOs are being formed top-down, with local leaders with political ambition paying off people and getting promoters and directors listed from their own coterie. SFAC is in a rush to approve new FPOs because the 10,000 target is looming. Surely, this was never the purpose of an FPO. Listening to them regularly is very important. Most of the mechanisms we see even for private companies are usually unidirectional. We don't collect enough information back up. A two-way information-gathering system is needed across the focus areas, whether it is their needs or actual data on what they are producing, their cost structure or their profits.

- **Pain points and sweet spots:** After understanding the key issues faced by the farmer, and looking at the available technologies, the sweet spot is quite clear. The dos and don'ts are important to understand. Right farmer segmentation, pricing, inducing trial and showing quick results with technologies, they can adopt and afford. If the technology has to do with crop cultivation itself, the government KVKs practise a two-crop cycle process before demonstrating to the farmer and before they adopt it. This must be kept in mind. The important point is to focus on the low-hanging fruit, where the impact can be quick and tangible, and to broadcast that far and wide so that success stories can be shared, and it leads to word-of-mouth adoption.

- **Choosing target audience:** To achieve the above, I believe that farmers across several states of varying dynamics, as well as farmers in the mid-holding range, should be chosen. Choosing solutions which involve groups and need collaboration as well as are easy to use but need farmer to be deeply involved will result in early success.

- **Production vs marketing vs advisory:** A crucial conclusion which gets borne out by the studies and interactions is that between the three major components, if one had to choose, most people believe that it should be the market output linkage and offtake piece. It is felt that improving production is easier and an internal task which can be handled. The second piece would be advisory and awareness of what is already available or happening. Focusing on actually improving production yield or reducing cost or choosing better crops which are more marketable should be lower in the priority. I do not fully agree with this, as I have outlined throughout this book. But the debate continues. The worry around focusing too much on production is that prices crash at the *mandis*, and the farmer will not make any profits even after achieving higher production, unless they have long-term offtake contracts in place.

- **A pathway to it all:** One of the important conclusions and messages of the book is to involve the farmer to give them a sense of ownership and that they have designed the solution or it is something they had asked for—a bottom-up approach rather than a top-down push down of schemes and products done by a multitude of agencies. Second, the farmer must feel that the service/product provider's interests are aligned to their own, which means including variable pricing and performance/outcome-linked fees wherever possible. This will also help in building trust and acceptance. Third, any sales cycle should involve detailed demos and trials or showcasing examples where the solution is working in live conditions. Two more things: A buy-in must be created by involving the youth as well as the women in the family. Let the whole family get involved. This will help in involving the youth too. Selling through extension advisors is also important. Finally, there must be a path to profits for the seller too, or in the case of the government itself, it has to be temporary, one-time support; otherwise, it will not be viable and hence will not carry through in the long term.

- **Celebrate and broadcast early wins of early adopters:** The best way to get this ball rolling is to focus on solutions which can be easily adopted and have high impact. Use these success stories then to celebrate them and most importantly broadcast them to a wider audience. It is an important conclusion of this book. We must use communication campaigns to spread the good word and educate. These mass campaigns are a must, whether done by private or public organizations.

- **No more schemes:** What I mean by this is that the supply of schemes and solutions keeps coming, but their take-up must be monitored more closely. In fact, I would say that there is no need to launch any new scheme. If just the penetration and usage of existing programmes improves even a little bit, a huge impact can be had, for example, the eNAM system. After some five years of its launch, still only about 11 per cent of India's farmers are signed up on the platform, and much less probably trade on it. There is a model law for land lease agreements since a few years as well, but most such arrangements are still undertaken verbally. I have not seen a single farmer tell me that he has even a panchayat-registered tenancy agreement. Similarly, contract farming model Act is in place since 2018, but still farmers, NGOs and FPOs are struggling to ensure offtake at a guaranteed price. Even a very valuable idea like that of short-term vocational training in agriculture (ACABC) since 2002 has trained about 75,000 students and supported 32,000 ventures. In about 20 years, 75,000 (implying about 3,000–4,000 per year across India) is not a very large number when India has 600 million rural youth. We must mobilize more training facilities and attract more students to join this very positive idea. Private players should also look at this very closely.

- **Never-ending request for grants:** I will take a little bold step here and put some blame on the farmers, FPOs and even NGOs, maybe because of the past habits or because of the way governments in general have for political or other reasons kept 'molly-coddling' the farmers, but the farmers have also become highly dependent on these support schemes. This has led to them as well as collective bodies like FPOs and even NGOs sometimes too easily or quickly asking for more financial assistance, and I feel that they could be more aggressive or assertive before building a case for more grants. One cannot blame the farmer for their risk appetite going down to almost zero after frequent droughts and loss of harvest or terrible price levels wiping out their income in recent years. But at least the NGOs, FPOs and extension officers should not run to the government at the drop of a hat. The other issue that rises here is that given the huge amount of very generous financial grants the governments already give to farmers and agriculture under various schemes, the system has also become self-fulfilling in the sense that unscrupulous elements have made it an industry of just tapping on every rupee available, and often the benefits of those funds are never seen by those who really need it.

- **Agritech is a two-way street:** Something that gets missed out in discussions on agritech but is a very useful point is that agritech is not just about farmers. Even the government needs to adopt it. The course on 'e-Learning on Digital Agriculture' run by the World Bank on edX highlights this point very well. As I mentioned above, the government needs to collect from-the-ground-up data and information for various purposes. This will be more efficient if technology is being used by the government right at the grassroots level. All the touch points that the government already has who regularly are in touch with the farmers (BDOs, KVKs, etc.) should be enabled with tablets or apps with which during their routine trips they can 'upload' a lot of invaluable information. This will also help the government get data on other areas such as stocks and inventory as well as acreage more efficiently. Second, there is a need to equip the extension officers with such gadgets too, so that they can perform their role of giving advice and taking inputs better.

- **Don't take my word for it!** Lastly, it is very important to note that a lot can be written or said about new technologies and the wonderful impact they are able to deliver to the farmer. But the proof of the pudding is in the eating. Much of the data on outcomes of various agritech offerings is mostly anecdotal. This is the case globally. Not many independently verified studies have been conducted. In fact, the impact of certain services like extension or equipment aggregation rentals is unproven. I strongly believe that as the agritech start-up ecosystem proliferates across rural India, the government via AUs should conduct such studies and publish factual result outcomes and distribute on a large scale. This will go a long way in building credibility of the offerings and also in a way protecting the farmers from not embracing things which are yet to be proven. It will also build the farmers' trust in the modern farming push. Agritech is only as good as its actual results, after all!

I hope that the readers have enjoyed reading this book on agribusiness and technology as much as I have done researching, preparing, travelling and talking to people for it. I will continue to have these conversations with the farmers as I look forward to the future of farming in India.

APPENDIX
MORE GROUND STORIES

THE SAVVY FARMER AND HIS WOES

Ravi is a mountain-trekking guide in the daytime and a third-generation farmer during his free time. This was a chance meeting for me. My wife and I signed up for a snow trek in the mountains near Shimla and got talking to our guide for the day. While most of the conversation of the course centred around the terrain we were going to confront that day and tips for dealing with such terrain, my curiosity took the better of me and I started digging deeper into the farming side of his life. It turned out that his grandfather was a full-time farmer, but his father took up a government job and hired a Nepali family to help him run the farm while he was away on work. It was when Ravi and his three brothers grew up that they thought to refocus on farming. Ravi and his younger brother spend more time on the farm than his two older brothers. He has been very keen to adopt mechanization, technology and best practices at his farm to improve yields and revenues and cut costs. He mainly has apple orchards but has also planted plums, apricots, peaches, pears, kiwis, pomegranates, persimmon, lettuce and asparagus. He said that he had been experimenting with different fruits and exotic vegetables to achieve an optimal mix. On the farm, they already use small tilling machines (in terrace, farming tractors cannot be used). He also uses power drills, chain saw and manual irrigation. He was amused at my questions and said that his father had gone to the market to look for a good weed-removing machine (a lot of stones on the field damage the blades and hence must have a robust one). He already also buys some inputs from online marketplaces and said that he in fact paid a premium for a brand he thought was more suitable for him! The biggest problems farmers face in hill areas, especially Himachal Pradesh, are water and the fact that newer apple farmers in the lower regions get an earlier harvest and can capture much better prices; short-term storage solutions, if available to local farmers from the upper reaches, will help them significantly improve realizations. We had almost reached our base camp for the trek, and I risked starting off without safety instruction from him. Hence, better sense prevailed, and I ended the conversation there. He signed off saying that he was always looking for ways to reduce his labour and other input cost and find solutions for his water shortage. It was some food for thought!

FROM ENGINEERING COLLEGE TO THE ORCHARD

I was camping out in the hills during early spring this year trying to get this book underway with the idea also to cover some hill states into my book field research rather than always only focusing on the 'cow belt' of the mainstream agricultural states. In fact, the hill states focus more on horticulture, which is something I wanted to cover in more details. It was also by luck that the local extension office of the government was just below my hotel. I walked in and introduced myself to the very young chief officer there and over a few cups of very hot and sweet spiced tea, we spent over an hour discussing the state of agriculture in his area. It was he who mentioned what has happened in his neighbouring areas since the last five–six years. There was a boom of engineering institutes run by private colleges. Young students enrolled in it, expecting a great career ahead. But when they graduated two–three years back, there were no jobs. Rather than to keep looking and waste even more time, some of them realized the opportunity which could be unearthed right in their own farms and orchards. There was a buzz about how apple prices were going up and new varieties could lead to better earnings. A cohort of some 80 engineers from that area got together and improved their knowledge and understanding and jumped into horticulture and haven't looked back since! It was also eye-opening that the government was very progressive and was giving high grants and subsidies, as much as 40–80 per cent, on important tools and equipment needed by farmers, whether it was fencing material to protect their farms from animals or netting to protect trees from the frost.

I was so amazed by listening to this story that I promptly told him how I intended to do more work around this trend and cover it in my book and that it would make interesting reading and I would call it the Himachal model, where positive vibes, government support and use of modern practices had created a virtuous cycle.

OF AGRITOURISM AND BROCCOLI

While continuing my field trip in Himachal Pradesh in December 2020, I spent a week doing meetings in a village called Andretta, some 50 km away from Palampur.

We were walking up one of the ubiquitous terraced fields one evening—in fact, running up—to catch the sunset which was rapidly disappearing behind the hills. We had to reach the top of this small hill to catch the stunning view before it set. We had to reach up in minutes. Halfway up, we came across a beautiful, terraced field—quite large compared to what we were seeing around us—and we stopped to take a closer look. We could see a variety of vegetables growing and many small sections carved out to grow a wide variety of crops. Mr Negi—a very urbane-looking person—stepped out of a large bungalow to greet us and ask us what we were looking for. We introduced ourselves, and I spoke to him about my interest in the subject of rural India and farming. He was very excited to hear about it and happily agreed to speak to me and answer my questions. In fact, he invited us in, introduced us to his wife and daughter and asked us to stay back for some tea! I told him that I wanted to catch the sun before it sets and would be right back and have a chat with him on my way down.

After we had caught one of the most stunning sunsets and taken dozens of pictures, we walked back down and sat down to speak to Mr Negi and his family. Here was a second-generation farmer who worked in the city of Delhi but came back home to tend to his farm every few months. He had recently expanded his farm by buying out the land adjoining it and expressed frustration that another piece which was equally large was unavailable, as the owners neither wanted to cultivate it nor sell it to him. Due to the lockdown, he was forced to spend several months in the village, and he decided to use it well and started experimenting—one thing he mentioned really stood out for me and made me think. He said that he was building another floor in his house which he would let out for agri-tourism/farm stays. I was quite taken aback with the progressive nature. He said that one must take a holistic view of farming and capitalize on the good weather and scenery in his village to increase avenues of making money. He also mentioned how he was experimenting with newer higher-yielding crops which they had never grown before but felt these would do well in terms of production, yields and prices. We were thrilled to see him growing broccoli and even more when his son (in his late 20s) came out and showed us grape trees he had grown around the periphery of his farm. We were stunned and very impressed with the enterprise this family was showing.

While we took our leave, after a nice hot cup of tea, and thanked them for their hospitality, he told us to visit them again and that his wife would love to cook some local traditional food for us to try. The foodie that my wife is, she would have taken them up for the offer was it not for our tight schedule.

ELECTRIC SCOOTERS ON THE FARM!

Kashyap Bhai and I missed each other on the phone a few times. Finally, we caught up just about 8 PM, and I thought that it would be a brief chat given we were heading into dinner time. When at 9 PM, I asked him I should let him go, he requested me to spend 10 more minutes, as he also had some questions for me! What about his dinner? I asked. He said, 'Sir, in the villages we eat just before sunset,' and that he had already completed his meal and was free if I was. Let's wind back a bit. He started telling me his story, which started about five years ago, when after spending about eight years in the family retail business he quit that routine and decided to take the plunge into farming.

He belonged to a village close to Ahmedabad, Gujarat. The family (his brother and father) had no prior history of agriculture. So he was going to do it from scratch. Help from farmers and the local AU helped him set off on this journey. He was praising the team at the AU with their short courses as well as farm visits they organized. He owned about 5 acres, and his focus of cultivation was organic and self-sufficiency. He hence grew grains (to sell) and vegetables as well as fruits for his family consumption. He had built underground rainwater harvesting tanks which last him a whole year. In fact, he thought of purchasing more land next door to build a pond for holding rainwater and raising the ground water level so that he could irrigate it better. He wasn't too much in favour of using machinery and preferred using hand-operated tools, but if he got electric vehicles for the farm, he would be more than happy to use it. He recently went to Uttar Pradesh when he heard of a farmer teaching new practices of keeping optimum distance between plants and to do multicropping, so that not only the farmer can get higher produce but also complementary crops enrich the soil and reduce or require no use of fertilizers. He told me that he was against taking any subsidies from the government. He would rather create a sustainable model: Was he for real or did someone just mirror so many of my thoughts? Indeed, I realized that change is happening, and we need few more such farmers to take the lead and spread the word. He went on to tell me about his children. His seven-year-old nephew was extremely curious about farming and was learning by visiting the farm regularly. His older daughter was pursuing a food and nutrition course but was less open to taking up direct agriculture. He said that children would do what they see their parents do. And teenagers already had a mind of their own. So we have to catch them early if we want them to be interested in agriculture. I told him about the ACABC courses offered by the government. He was all ears. When I thanked him and promised him to meet him when travel is safe, he asked me to remember and share the details about the ACABC scheme. I realized how important that last-mile information linkage was even for the most progressive farmer.

80 PER CENT FARMERS USE THE ENGLISH LANGUAGE APP!

I had connected with a few large agritech start-ups during this journey and wanted to share an interesting conversation here. Mr Mahesh was doing very well in a corporate career for the last 10–15 years but felt like taking up an agritech start-up challenge and quit his job to start a pan-India precision farming company. He calls it the brain of the farm, focusing on becoming a decision support system for the farmer where important and risky decisions are left to the intuition of the farmer. His company has an integrated solution with hardware (device) and software to study below-and above-the-ground data and analytics and shares the actionable conclusions with the farmer. That's when I asked him, 'What about the language?' He said that his company was operating in seven states and offered all the seven languages. But to even his own surprise, he said that 80 per cent of the farmers operating the

25,000 acres that his company currently works with used the English language app without any local language interfaces! Indeed, something heartening and surprising! It is a very encouraging reality from the ground. We were discussing in more details his choice of horticultural farmers. I told him that my research findings point to the fact that horticultural farmers are more open to change and so his choice was a good one. He told me that I was bang on and that was really what they were seeing as well, leading to a faster adoption of their solutions once they focus on a cluster approach to address groups of farmers growing the same crop—targeted segmentation as we talk about in the book as well.

PAALA KARNA: LEARNING THE ART OF MIXING THINGS UP

Jayesh works for an agribusiness which focuses on warehousing, financial services as well as running an online marketplace. The company reaches about 200,000 farmers—about 80 per cent via FPOs and the rest directly. While bulk of their business is B2B, a tenth comes from directly connecting the farmer with the buyers. After playing a lot of phone tag, I was finally able to connect with him and had an hour-long conversation. After much effort of addressing potential disputes in a trade, the company was seeing a good take-up on their platform. I was told that it was not just quality but also allowing multiple parameters for listing, ability to negotiate price, safe payment mechanism with an earnest money deposit and finally a very detailed dispute settlement mechanism which addressed all sorts of disputes. All this is still worth it, he said as 'the platform makes 0.25–0.5 per cent vs about 4 per cent that the *mandi* and its agents charge'. Basically, these savings are shared between the buyer, seller and the platform. And everyone benefits. 'Wow! That's like a no-brainer,' I said. 'How do you spread the good word?' Jayesh told me that they used voice bytes, WhatsApp, social media and opinion leaders to share such success stories. The news must be spreading like fire if farmers are able to make 5–10 per cent more without spending anything. That is when Jayesh explained to me that they had a strict quality control applied based on buyer requirements, and hence farmers could sell only a portion of their best grade crop and had to return to the *mandis* to offload all their produce. I had heard this before—more from the farmers' side—that they were not clear of the benefit if they would have to run to the buyer of last resort (the *mandi*). I was not willing to give up and kept probing Jayesh. It was deep into lunch time by now on a Saturday afternoon, and I was feeling guilty, but Jayesh was more than happy to continue this conversation. He told me that the reason *mandis* can buy everything is because they do a *paala*, meaning a mixture of all grades of the crop, and are able to still sell at a higher price to the buyer (e.g., A, B and C grades mixed to sell as B+ grade). Ah! Now I get it. So why can't your company do the same? Well, it is a very operationally heavy task and needs a lot of labour and time. 'What about the eNAM then?' I asked. It had 17 million farmers on it after all! Jayesh said that most farmers were unlikely to even know they were on it. It was a lot of *mandi* sub-aggregators and traders putting existing offline trades online. I noticed that he was not very comfortable with this subject, so I took my cue and moved to the next topic quickly.

So the other way to address this is to get into a 'contract' with the farmer so that the buyers can 'control' the quality of the crop at all stages, via extension services (crop choice, seed, fertigation optimization, timing of sowing and harvesting, etc.) Why not do that? I asked. Jayesh told me that it was exactly the solution: to use rich extension services along with the output market linkages and in fact get into more tighter contract arrangements. They were in fact doing a pilot on it. Another thing Jayesh said was that even when they were able to buy a lot more from the farmers, on-the-ground collection centres and warehouses were needed at district and tehsil levels. Otherwise, any one entity even after years would barely cover half a per cent of a state's farmer population. It would take decades to achieve scale and wide penetration. That's why broader marketing of success stories could create more dissonance, if the infrastructure was not available 'as advertised'. And we surely don't want that. It was time for me to wrap up the discussion, and I asked him two things which could make a difference—it felt like he was waiting to share his thoughts with me on this! He said that a PPP model was a must—and I agree and have heard this from several other players. He gave an example of National Agricultural Cooperative Marketing Federation of India (NAFED) partnering with private players to extend the primary procurement centres to every tehsil level, so that more farmers could join the network. Second, he felt that even if the existing *mandis* just fix one thing—pricing and payment according to proper grading—the *mandi* system itself could become a much better marketplace where the farmer has an incentive to provide higher-quality produce. Third, he said that mini-storage solutions for farmers should be built nearer to their farms. Capacity of 500–1,000 metric tonnes is enough. Doesn't the government already have a scheme for this? He said that it had been there on paper with not much of build-out yet. He said that private companies were now coming into this space as well. I felt that the surge in FPOs would at least help such entrepreneurs gather volume for these mini warehouses, and Jayesh agreed to that.

This experience confirmed my views that most agritech companies are focusing either on pre-harvest or post-harvest. No one is focusing on the entire value chain. And, second, that the core value add can only happen if one starts at the seed and crop level with rich real-time advisory, rather than just focusing on input or output marketplace.

NEVER HEARD OF COMPETITION FROM EXTENSION SERVICE OFFICERS

A short conversation with one of the founders of a large agritech start-up threw up this interesting reaction from Mr Shailesh. I had asked him how they dealt with farmers while selling their advisory services when they brought up the 'competition'—the local government-friendly neighbourhood extension officer? 'I have never heard any farmer tell me about other extension services they are getting' Even if they do, it is very basic and district-level information. While what is needed is field-level and even intra-farm. This was a company operating across seven–eight states, with over half a million active user farmers directly on their platform. Their core activity was integrated input marketplace, deep farm advisory and output marketplace, all rolled into one. I was curious about the openness of the farmer towards the high-tech advisory service they offered. Shailesh admitted that the way to go was to first focus on helping them with their existing crop rather than trying to suggest major crop selection changes. They are less open to that. Once trust is built by cheaper inputs, better realizations and free advisory services, one can start advocating bigger changes. I thought that it was the right thing to do and in line with my thinking on 'low-hanging fruits' and the 'sweet spot'. Shailesh further explained to me how they handled the logistics on both the sides. They had about 2,000 micro-entrepreneurs who covered all villages in a 3–5-km radius and act as the offline component. It was at their centres that farmers came to collect inputs or deposit their produce. Basic weighing and moisture content was measured, and a weighted average price for their produce was paid to them. The company then moved this to their larger hub storage centres, where they further sorted, graded, dried and packaged the produce to ship it to their buyers. I asked him that weren't the FPOs already beginning to do this as well. He said, 'Only a very small fraction of them is doing this service as of now, maybe 3–4 per cent only.'

Finally, I asked him what he felt was needed to accelerate agritech take-up. He was quick in responding as if he had answered this question many times before! He said that three things were needed. First, further deepening of telecommunication networks and smartphone penetration which is the backbone of delivery. Second, more agritech players attacking from different directions is in itself a big solution and hence government support is needed to encourage them. Third, the India AgriStack the government had announced recently would reduce a lot of the prelim tasks for start-ups, giving them data and insights, and help in faster acquisition and onboarding of farmers. Otherwise, he said, sometimes companies spend years only to later find out that they were looking at or for the wrong thing!

It was a short and punchy meeting, I thought. One of the few 'supermarkets' of agritech offering all the parts of the value chain, including financing help and advisory, a one-stop shop for the farmer, will address our key pathway—early adoption and high impact.

WHERE ARE THE BIRDS?

When I shared the news about my second book with some of my close friends on a group chat, one of them privately messaged me and told me that he has many friends and relatives in farming and that I must speak to a few of them if I was not yet done with my research work. I told him that I would continue to have conversations with farmers even after my book gets published, as this would keep me updated and add to my anecdotal library. So I was more than happy to speak to more farmers. I got in touch with one large farming family of Uttar Pradesh, and this is the story I heard. PK, as he is known to friends, was a third-generation farmer but went and did his engineering. He never pursued it though and has been involved with livelihood solutions for very small farmers in the Uttar Pradesh area all his career, including eco-tourism initiatives. His main point was that marketing linkage was the key challenge where more focus was needed. He told me how farmers in that belt used to grow potatoes and rape seeds. He focused on the core cultivation decisions and after all agronomic tests and data, and a pilot on a 12-acre farm, he showed them and convinced them that they could grow the traditional yellow mustard as well as sesame as an additional crop and actually—hold your breath—even olives! Yes, olives! PK got special varieties from Israel, mastered the drip irrigation process and was ready with his idea. He was careful to not jeopardize what the farmers were already growing and only focused on either additional crop in the lean season via irrigation or using ridge farming to grow olive trees on the side. He formed a 600-farmer FPO (about 40,000 acres) and is all set to nearly triple their incomes in 3–5 years (from ₹30,000 per year per acre to ₹115,000). He plans to set up processing infrastructure to make olive green tea and olive as well as sesame oil. He already has a brand ready and starting discussions with potential buyers. He also has his eyes set on growing grapes for wine and a bee farm to make honey. It is a classic copybook diversification on the farm! If all this sounds hunky-dory, it was not an easy task to convince the farmers to even start the FPO. Most would not give him even their Aadhaar cards, worried that it is another government scheme, or someone would steal their land! His main challenge now is how the buyers would shift from 'imported' olive oil to a local one, and it may be a slow process and would need lower pricing. We then also talked about exportability of his produce and high fertilizer and pesticide residues. He assured me that he was only using organic items and manure. But that's when he recalled an old incident he saw while travelling in Punjab—he was in the middle of large farms but there was not a sound of a bird. Is it not the countryside he thought to himself then? Then why are the farms so quiet? He later found out that the answer laid in high fertilizer and pesticide use. No bird wanted to be anywhere near it! And that was decades ago! While this remains a big issue (India's fertilizer consumption has jumped to 175 kg per acre from 2 kg in the last 70 years!), my other worry was how we could have more FPOs managed by such entrepreneurial people!

AMAZON AND ITS EFFECT ON INDIAN FARMING

Jacob is an agripreneur in Kerala. He has been involved with the grassroots since 2013 and has hence seen a lot of challenges and opportunities that agriculture has to offer in his state. He has himself dabbled in cultivation a few times—cardamom and even strawberries!

He started off by highlighting to me some basic differences in the farming culture in Kerala. Unlike other southern states such as Tamil Nadu, Andhra Pradesh and Karnataka, in Kerala, farmers are used to more long-duration plantations such as rubber and spices. They plant the crop, wait for 5–7 years and then enjoy the 'fruits' for the next 25. This leads to much lower propensity to try short cycle crops in general. The second issue is of very high use of pesticides and fertilizers to make the produce look acceptable (e.g., the right colour and shape of cardamom). But eventually it gets rejected due to the high residue. In fact, the cardamom belt in Udichi apparently does not have a single snake! It is only because of this. The problem is so intense that once he tried to grow cardamoms there with a very environment-friendly way on a 5-acre plot—and his methods stood no chance against the heavy chemicals being used all around him—and he suffered a major pest attack and lost a lot of money! However, he sees some positives emerging. A lot of engineers and natives working in the Middle East are coming back due to lesser opportunities, and even in India, due to the proliferation of Amazon, just starting a trading or small retail business is no longer viable. Hence, they often have no choice but to turn to agriculture. Also, many such well-educated people are trying new techniques, especially in the area of water harvesting, scientific farm decision-making and more organic and sustainable agriculture. So much, in fact, that Jacob now sees a lot of demand for his 'end-to-end consulting' services. But he felt that the FPOs had a big role to play. Management skills at FPOs are very crucial, as older farmers are very averse to using new technology and think that they know everything. It is hence a tough task to convince them to join a group and adopt new practices. Another issue is that even when farmers are open-minded, the control and grip of the input companies are so strong that they find it difficult to escape that. He felt that the farmers need to have a business model in place. While I thanked Jacob for his time, he told me that he was now starting an NGO which would set up a few hundred kiosks across the state which would be a one-stop shop to provide advisory to farmers' sustainable farming including testing their soil. These kiosks would also supply inputs which are organic. I wished him all the best for his new venture, and he promised to introduce me to a few farmers across Kerala, which he promptly did.

AND SOME FPOs GET STUCK

John worked for an FPO for three years in Karnataka. It had 1,000 farmer with about 6 acres each. While the nearby belt was full of fruits such as papaya and pomegranate (4,000–5,000 acres), their farmer cluster was growing pulses mainly with some jowar and bajra too. The area was arid and heavily dependent on rains with no irrigation facilities. His own farm of about 8 acres was not yielding any results and, with less time on his hands, he let it out for just ₹3,000 per acre per year, much lower than the ₹10,000–₹15,000 I had heard from other parts of the country. I asked him why he let it out for so little? He said that his land was dry and not irrigated. He is the only one in the family to run it and with his FPO job, he had no time. He was not earning much more than ₹3,000 anyway. He had done a proper agreement in writing which I believe is the result of fully digitized land records in Karnataka. We turned our discussion to his experience at the FPO. He said that he had left it and now joined a sustainable agriculture-focused NGO. The old FPO wound up after he left. Of the three years he worked, with his salary of ₹11,000 per month, he had to even bear his own transportation costs but even so, the whole year three years he did not get paid at all. The board of directors apparently did not have much interest, as they had other businesses, and now the FPO was stuck since the last six months. All the good work he did seems to be going waste. He had helped the FPO procure four tractors and a spraying machine and had even got the farmers a very good fruits and groundnuts contract where they avoided the middlemen and farmers got the full price even if there was 2–3 per cent wastage. His voice had a sense of pride and remorse, I felt—pride in what he did and remorse that he could not see it through in a bigger way. His voice brightened up when I asked him about what he does now. He said that they had selected 350 farmers from the village via the panchayat and were training them in environment-friendly best practices of using less chemicals and fertilizers as well as practising Zero Budget Natural Farming (ZNBF) with cow dung, cow urine, neem cakes, etc. A qualified MSc in agriculture was doing the sessions for the farmers. He told me that he was actually on a farm for one such training session that day and promised to send me pictures. Within an hour, I got a few pictures from him. He sounded so excited about his new project and assignment. I also ended this meeting with a bittersweet feeling. This was not the first time I was hearing of such stories of failure (Bihar was another), but the undying enthusiasm of people like John is what put a smile back on my face too.

ABOUT THE AUTHOR

Sujit Sahgal is a financial markets professional with over 28 years of experience in various investment banks in India and rest of Asia. Over the years, his area of work has included macroeconomics, investment strategy, sector and company research, equity sales as well as investing globally across asset classes. He completed his MBA in 1993 and has spent most of his working career based in Singapore, having recently returned to India.

During his research days, he was ranked number 1 analyst for global IT services research by Institutional Investor. He was also consistently ranked as a top-three analyst in Asia by Asiamoney and Institutional Investor. Among various financial institutions, he has spent close to a decade with UBS AG and ran his own global macro, multi-strategy hedge fund from Singapore for a few years. He has been with HSBC since 2010 and is currently the head of institutional equities for HSBC India.

He is the author of the book *A Wall Street View of Rural India: A Banker's Diary of a Decade of Road Trips* (June 2020). The book captures his observations, insights and views emanating from nearly a dozen rural trips done over the last 10 years across 7–8 states of India and meeting hundreds of farmers covering close to a hundred villages. The trips included 300–400 foreign investors from over 10 countries who were trying to gauge the overall health of the rural economy, which is such an important part of India.

Apart from his interests in the financial markets and rural India, he is a travel and trekking enthusiast. He is a serious poet of Urdu and writes under the pen name Haasil.

He regularly recites in mushairas and Urdu literature festivals all over India and internationally. His first collection of Urdu ghazals and nazms is under preparation to be published soon. He also loves horseback riding, skiing and a round of golf in his free time.

He is married to his college sweetheart of 32 years and has two sons, who are working overseas. He currently lives in Mumbai, with his wife and the love of their life, their yellow Labrador__Cheers!

STAY ENCOURAGED • STAY CREATIVE • STAY MOTIVATED

Keep abreast of the most cutting-edge thinking driving businesses today.

   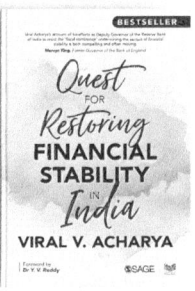

For special offers on these books and more visit **stealadeal.sagepub.in** — **Steal A Deal** YOUR ONE-STOP-SHOP FOR LOWEST PRICE

www.sagepub.in